Ten Minutes a Week to Great Meetings

and

The Meeting Idea Book

By Joel Levitt

Springfield Resources
www.MeetingDefender.com

A full catalog record for this book will be available from the Library of Congress
ISBN: 978-1-4827-7675-1

By Joel Levitt
Edited by Nancy Boxer

Quantity sales: Special discounts are available for purchases
by organizations.
For information, please contact Sales@MeetingDefender.com

Individual sales:
This book is available from www.MeetingDefender.com

College, University sales: If you would like to use this book in an
educational setting, please contact Sales@MeetingDefender.com

10   9   8   7   6   5   4   3   2

Table of Contents

Other books by Joel Levitt

Facilities Management, Managing Maintenance for Buildings and Facilities (Momentum Press, NY 2013) www.momentumpress.net

The Complete Handbook of Preventive and Predictive Maintenance, Second Edition (Industrial Press, NY 2011) www.Industrialpress.com

Basics of Fleet Maintenance (MROzone, Ft Meyers, FL 2010) www.MRO-Zone.com

Maintenance Planning, Scheduling and Coordination, Second Edition by Don Nyman and Joel Levitt (Industrial Press, NY 2010) www.Industrialpress.com

TPM Reloaded (Industrial Press, NY 2010) www.Industrialpress.com

Handbook of Maintenance Management, Second Edition (Industrial Press, NY 2009) www.Industrialpress.com

Lean Maintenance (Industrial Press, NY 2008) www.Industrialpress.com

Managing Factory Maintenance, Second Edition (Industrial Press, NY 2004) www.Industrialpress.com

Managing Maintenance Shutdowns and Outages (Industrial Press, NY 2004) www.Industrialpress.com

Acknowledgements

First and foremost I would like to thank my life partner, Nancy Boxer, who not only championed this work but also spent hours editing the various drafts. She lent great insight to the whole process and always smiled even when I made unreasonable demands.

I sent a draft to a few people in my inner circle and got some great suggestions. They include my childhood friend and executive in non-profits for 30 years Jonathan P. Harmon. His training in both meetings and psychology were very helpful in developing some of the themes.

Another helpful set of comments came from my son, Andrew who is a project manager and is a self-professed meeting lover. In my consulting field, Rona Palmer, a marketing director for a software company reminded me of some of our mandatory meetings. Eric Houston from SKF also cheered me on. Comments from Jeff Finesilver, Don Sapatkin and Martha Lask were also helpful.

Some of my own training in effective meetings came from Landmark Education, specifically their Team Management and Leadership Programs. We had many meetings that were run from a set of principles that I have now, after many years, internalized.

This work started as an adjunct to my training in large factory and refinery shutdowns, where meetings are essential. Many of the ideas come from those students over the years. In particular, the training I present for Life Cycle Institute in Charleston, South Carolina, has been pivotal to this material.

Thanks.

Joel Levitt, *2013*

Meeting FAQ:
Quick Answer Locator to Common Meeting Management questions

• How do I get people to read the reports we will be discussing?	Chapter 3 Meeting Culture and Ground Rules, Setting ground rules
• How do I get quiet people to talk? (Sometimes they have the best ideas)	Chapter 3 Meeting Culture and Ground Rules, Setting ground rules
• Would an agenda help me? How?	Chapter 4 Agenda and Subject Matter
• What is the best way to keep people on topic subject?	Chapter 3 Meeting Culture and Ground or Rules, Setting ground rules, Facilitation: Running a productive meeting
• Who was Roberts and why do we follow his Rules Order?	Chapter 2 Types of Meetings –Formal of Meetings
• Will having ground rules make a difference?	Chapter 3 Meeting Culture and Ground Rules, Setting ground rules
• I get a headache from our meetings. Is there anything I can do?	Chapter 1 Some background about meetings, 7 Symptoms of Bad Meetings and What to Do
• I have trouble keeping track of the details; can I automate this?	Chapter 13 Using Outlook to help Manage Meetings
• How should the agenda be organized?	Chapter 4 Agenda and subject matter
• What to do about disruptive people in the meeting that I just want to punch out? Why do people act that way?	Chapter 11 Destructive Meeting Symptoms
• How do I keep people from falling asleep?	Chapter 4 Agenda and Subject Matter, Circadian rhythm
• I want my meetings to be efficient, yet I also want people to get to know each other and feel friendly.	Chapter 3 Meeting culture and ground rules 39, Big Check List

continued

Meeting FAQ Continued

• Why don't people change their minds once they are wrong?	Chapter 10 Advanced facilitation, see they Dissonance
• What would be in an initial meeting checklist?	Chapter 7 The Use of Checklists
• How do we handle bad news at a meeting?	Chapter 8 Facilitation: Running a productive meeting, What to do with big news
• We have a lot of problem solving meetings. Are they any different than regular meetings?	Chapter 9 Facilitating the Problem-solving Meeting
• I just took on being secretary for my organization. What should I do?	Chapter 5 Notes and Minutes
• Is there a way to have very short, very specific meetings?	Chapter 2 Types of meetings –Flash Meetings
• Seriously, how can we really, concretely improve our meetings – no bull and no extra stuff to buy!	10 Minutes a week to great Meetings
• Where can I find tons of ideas to help improve my meetings?	Big Checklist of ideas
• Do you have other resources or articles where I can find out more?	Bibliography
• Why should we spend the time writing up the minutes when we'll remember the important stuff anyway?	Chapter 5 Minutes and Notes Memory effect
• Is there any technology or easy techniques to help take the minutes?	Chapter 5 Minutes and Notes
• Can't we just stop having meetings?	Chapter 1 Some background about meetings, Decision Point: Is this meeting actually necessary?

continued

Meeting FAQ Continued

• What can I do about jokesters?	Chapter 3 Meeting culture and ground rules, Chapter 8 Facilitation: Running Effective Meetings
• I'm not biased but the other people are.	Chapter 10 Advanced facilitation, Unconscious bias
• Do you have a layout or template for minutes?	Chapter 5 Minutes
• How do I shut people up who talk too much or repeat themselves?	Chapter 3 Meeting culture and ground rules, Chapter 8 Facilitation: Running Effective Meetings
• How should we deal with lateness?	Chapter 3 Meeting culture and ground rules
• Is there a way to organize reminders for actions promised?	Chapter 14 Using Outlook to help Manage Meetings
• What kind of skills do I need to run a good meeting?	Chapter 6 Roles people play (in meetings), Chapter 8 Facilitation: Running a productive meeting, Chapter 10 Advanced Facilitation
• How much do our meetings actually cost us? How can we cut this down?	Chapter 15 Using Meeting Defender software to improve meetings
• How do we deal with people taking phone calls during meetings?	Chapter 3 Meeting culture and ground rules
• How do I deal with people surfing the net or texting during meetings?	Chapter 3 Meeting culture and ground rules

Letter of introduction from Joel Levitt,
author, trainer and consultant

Since 1980 I have been the President of Springfield Resources. Springfield Resources is committed to helping our client organiza-tions treat their employees, their communities and the environment with respect.

We are management consultants in a wide variety of industries including pharmaceuticals, oil, mining, airports, hospitals, high tech manufacturing, school systems and utility companies. Springfield Resources has worked in private, public and governmental organizations as well as in highly regulated, unregulated, union and non-union environments.

We are considered one of the leading trainers in physical asset management throughout the US, Canada, Persian Gulf region, Europe, Australia and Asia and have trained over 17,000 professionals in 21 countries in more than 500 classes and workshops. Over 98% of our students rate the training very good or excellent.

Prior to founding Springfield Resources, I was a senior consultant at Computer Cost Control Corporation, where I designed computerized management systems for organizations including FedEx, United Airlines, JFK Airport, BFI, etc.

I have written ten books on industrial and organizational management and contributed chapters to many others. I have written over 100 articles for trade publications on a variety of management topics. You can expect a great deal of information, real-life examples, and successful practices from organizations around the world in my work, all delivered in an enjoyable, easily accessible style.

Thank you for reading.

Joel Levitt, *President*

I welcome your comments, which may be sent to
JDL@Maintrainer.com.

LESSONS for
The Meeting Idea Book

*Follow these lessons each week for 10 weeks
and see the results in better meetings,
increased effectiveness and greater job satisfaction.*

How to use this program

This program is easy to use. It can be initiated by management but must be adopted and hopefully really taken on by the team. We say "hopefully really taken on" because this is medicine that will prevent many of the adverse symptoms and after-effects of bad meetings that harm and hinder the participants. It is the participants who will immediately benefit, though the organization will ultimately benefit as well. Like many things that are good for you, this program requires practice and tenacity.

The first step is for participants to agree on the importance of improving the meeting. Building a case for improving a meeting might be as easy as stating the obvious, that the meetings can be wasteful and change would make everyone's life better.

The second step is for participants to review the material and agree to a several week trial. The group does not have to agree to the whole program. Much benefit can be derived from just 4 or 5 lessons. Have participants read these lessons, one each week, do their best to put each new lesson into practice at meetings for that week, and at the end of the initial trial period, decide if the benefit is worth the time and effort to continue.

Ideally each week's meetings will include a short discussion of the lesson topic for the week at the beginning of the meeting and a short discussion at the end of the meeting to introduce the topic for the following week.

It is possible (and desirable in some cases) to slow the program down to one topic every other week or even once a month. This might allow better digestion of the topic before moving on to the next one. Just keep it on the agenda and keep improving your approaches and understandings.

Everyone participates and gets to read the lesson of the week. In the beginning, at least, the extra work of incorporating these new lessons falls on the chair. But in fact, a successful meeting has a great deal to do with the cooperation of all the participants. If the meeting goes off topic, for example, it would be great if several participants notice it, having been sensitized to such infractions by reading about them, and help steer the group's focus back onto the agenda.

What is it about meetings?

If you ever want to get a groan of recognition from a group in business, non-profit or public service, just say something negative about meetings. Most people generally dislike and distrust organizational meetings.

For example, have you ever been to a meeting to "gather input" about a topic to help management make a decision, only to find the decision has already been made?

How about a meeting where the chair pontificates and generally dominates the discussion?

Have you ever looked around during a meeting and seen that half or more of the others are attending to other business, sleeping, texting, checking email, or just daydreaming?

The challenge is to take an entrenched institutional culture like you have with meetings, and mix it up, making them more relevant and faster paced. Imagine a day when people look forward to your meetings because they add wings to their productive efforts at the organization. Wouldn't this be worth 10 minutes a week for a few weeks in order to get there?

Lesson 1

*One simple idea that has saved billions and
what It could do for your meetings*

Reference: Meeting Improvement Idea Book, Chapter 7

We all know that checklists are widely used in settings where the outcome is critical (aviation, power plants, medicine or military operations). What we might not know is that the use of checklists has been proven useful in widely different situations. From industrial production floors to day care centers to political campaigns, checklists play a prominent role in keeping things moving safely and smoothly.

The idea is simple: Design a meeting checklist, distribute, post and use it. Here are a few tried and true simple rules to make it work best.

- The list should be on a single side of paper. Use a large font that is easy to read.
- The most effective checklists are short and quickly completed. Many can be run through in under a minute.
- The most effective checklists would typically have 7-10 or so items on them.
- Post the checklist and use it!

A checklist is simply a reminder system. It consists of things that you already know should be done but might forget one or two items during the course of an event. The checklist keeps the practices that make a successful meeting listed right there in front of you. That way even if you are tired, have a headache or are preoccupied, just keep consulting the checklist and you won't miss anything important.

You can also use the checklist to remind yourself to try new ideas, techniques or practices. For example you could rotate items into the list that you would like to try out, including some of the more unusual the items in the meeting idea list in the E-book Meeting Improvement Idea Book.

The power of the checklist is in the execution. It only has positive effect if used!

The items on your checklist could be further divided into sub-checklists, particularly for tasks which should be done prior to the meeting. You may want to create sub-lists for tasks to be done days before the meeting, right before, during, right after and after the meeting. This is done where there are more crucial tasks than the recommended 7-10 items, and they are distinct for some organizational reason. Airplane pilots have used different checklists for decades, with specific sub-lists for each step in flying (preflight, landing, emergency procedures, etc.).

For our purposes we can start by keeping the meeting checklist as simple as possible. These are living documents. We do want the checklists to grow smarter over time. They get smarter by incorporating new issues that occur and removing old solutions that no longer apply.

Idea for action: *An excellent idea is to use Meeting Defender Meeting Calculator to sample your meeting to get some baseline data which will be very useful later in the process.*

You can start with this checklist form and adapt it for your type and style of meetings. If you decide you do not want to do an item, remove it from your checklist!

Meeting Checklist		Title of meeting:		
Purpose of meeting:				
Date:	Facility:		Ad hoc?	Scheduled
Done	When	Idea to improve meeting		
	Few days before meeting	Have agenda sent out well before meeting with meeting day, time, location objective and topics, arrange catering if any		
	Few days before meeting *and* maybe the day before the meeting	Remind people who have promised to complete some work for the meeting.The reminder should be at the top of the communication (like the email) and made bold so it is very hard to miss.		
	10-20 minutes before meeting	Check that: • Room is actually available. • Check to see if the room is clean, • Easel has paper (if needed), white board is there, with markers, • Any other aids (like pens and pads), catering • Check out the AV before the meeting. Verify connections (Laptop to LCD projectors and thumb drives) are useable on the computer in the conference room. • You have the latest presentations, graphs, charts • Printed materials are complete and enough are printed		
	Just before the meeting starts	Assign (or request) someone to take minutes (who is good at it).		
	Beginning of the meeting	Have people introduce themselves and their role if people don't already know everyone. *People come in the door with a variety of concerns and preoccupations. Start the meeting by asking if anyone has any concerns or worries that will interfere with concentrating on the business at hand.*		
	Throughout the meeting	When you assign tasks and responsibilities, be sure to include in the minutes who is to carry out what and by when (Who-What-By when).		
	At the end of the meeting	The chair should wrap up the meeting with a summary of any agreements or assignments of tasks, plus any agreement for futhure meetings, etc.		
		At the end of the meeting ask people if the meeting achieved the objectives and to write down any ideas for improvement. (Note: Use survey form from Lesson 7)		

Lesson 2
Establish Ground Rules

Reference: Meeting Improvement Idea Book, Chapter 3

The dictionary defines a ground rule as "a basic rule of procedure or behavior." Taken together, the ground rules are important because they regulate conduct in a way that makes meetings work better.

Ground rules set up the limits and boundaries of behavior allowable at the meeting. Everyone gives up a little freedom of action in exchange for enhanced cooperation. Now in some circles, giving up any freedoms at all seems like a bad idea. But most people find that operating with these limits makes the meeting more productive and more satisfying overall. The ground rules chosen as a starting point tend to be a formalization of good business etiquette and plain good manners.

You want to pick and choose ground rules that suit your organization and meeting culture. At the outset, all meeting participants need to agree to abide by the ground rules. Ground rules for running a lawyer's deposition meeting would be very different from a kid's soccer league's meetings or a volunteer organization's board meetings. Even within the same industry, ground rules which work well in one corporation may be too stiff or too informal for another. If a rule gets in the way of a successful meeting then it should be banished from the list.

Of course, in the real world, people will often forget the agreement, and in the heat of discussion, forget the guidelines. Also in the real world people may argue about the meaning, plead that they didn't "really" agree, and try to get out of their agreement. The Chair may occasionally need to remind people of particular rules to restore order to the process. But once the rules have been in place for a while, participants tend to keep each other in check.

You might review the ground rules a few times in the beginning of a new meeting series or when someone new starts to attend. Also if there is an especially egregious incident of forgetting (or ignoring) the ground rules, the entire group should review them out loud at the beginning of the next meeting or two.

There are hundreds of potentially useful rules to choose from. Consider choosing a dozen or so and add or remove a few as issues arise and the group's meeting culture develops. Remember to review the ground rules at your kick off meeting and get everyone's agreement to abide by this particular set of rules.

Some ground rules to consider for a starting list:

Add to My List	GROUND RULES FOR MEETING	
1	Set up a focus: Everyone knows what this meeting is trying to accomplish. There might even be a mission statement and a statement how this particular meeting fulfills that mission.	
2	Agenda: Distribute an agenda before the meeting	
3	RSVP: Accept or decline invitations to the meeting, then show up if you accept. Communicate with chair or secretary if an emergency comes up after you say you are coming.	
4	Timing: Start and end on time	
5	Homework: Everyone comes assignments orreports to the Chair why they were not able to complete their assignment before the next meeting.	
6	Attention: Phones set to vibrate, text and email answered outside the room if urgent. No social sites, emailed jokes or random surfing allowed.	
7	Courtesy: Only the Chair can interrupt a speaker (and then only to bring the conversation back to the agenda or help manage the discussion).	
8	Focus: Discuss only the topic on the floor. All topics to be discussed are on the agenda.	
9	Participation: Every participant participates to the extent of his or her abiity and is encouraged to participate	
10	Follow-up: Keep minutes and action lists. All participants should have access to these documents.	

Lesson 3
Use your agenda as the map and packing list for the trip

In the field of planning we say that an hour of effective planning cuts the execution time of whatever job you are working on by 3-5 hours. This is on a one-on-one basis (1 labor hour of planning cuts 3-5 labor hours for one person). The justification for spending time planning your meetings is that this wasted time will be multiplied by the number of people in the room. Thus an hour of time spend in planning for a good meeting will generally result in real savings of 15-50 labor hours, depending on the number of people attending the meeting.

Reference: Meeting Improvement Idea Book, Chapter 4.

Goal

The goal of this lesson is to get you to take a few minutes making notes about what the meeting will cover and what it supposed to accomplish. This is important for any meeting but particularly important for ad hoc meetings. Scheduled meetings may have an invisible agenda by tradition (i.e. we've always covered these items in this order), and thus may need less planning time.

Spur of the moment meetings are frequently useful but may result in a lot of wasted effort, especially if the goals and outcomes of the meeting are not clear. Ad hoc meetings spring up like mushrooms after a storm. It is essential for the leader to spend a few minutes before calling people together, thinking through the reason for the meeting and the topics to be covered.

Before the meeting gets started – save time by telling everyone where and when the meeting will be held!

The agenda should have all the logistical information for the meeting, including time, place and any other information needed to attend. If there are reports to read ahead of time, actions you promised to report on, reports to give or decisions to think about, they all should be printed clearly on the agenda. Clarity beforehand will prevent people from showing up at the wrong time and place, or people not having done their homework.

Other possible items to include on the agenda:
- *People expected to be in attendance*

The leader should know who will not be attending from among expected participants. Taking roll call might be the first official business.
- *Logistics and timing of the meeting*

Where the meeting is being held (along with door entry codes, physical addresses (for GPS if people are traveling in), and other specifics. Also note on agenda if food or beverages will be served. Include the time the meeting starts and the latest time it will end.

- *Reasons for the meeting and what you are trying to accomplish.*
- *Topics to be covered*

Of course any topic can be covered that is relevant to the group. Some of the categories could include some of the items below.

- *Reports from accountability holders*
- *Old business*
- *New business*
- *Decisions*
- *Reviews*
- *Reports to be given, results to be reviewed*
- *You may want to attach the minutes from the last meeting to the agenda and links to any material to be reviewed.*

Agenda timing: It is far better to plan 45 minutes of work for a 1-hour slot (and let people out early) then it is to plan an hour's worth of work for a 45 minute slot and keep people late.

Lesson 4
Structures for managing action

Reference: Meeting Improvement Idea Book, Chapter 5

Actions to be undertaken, decisions to be made, education to be passed on and communications of all the above are the core reasons to meet. Without intentional action, most meetings are a complete waste of time.

In this usage a structure is an automatic method of reminding people about any action they promised at the last meeting. An example of a structure is to take the action items form the meeting and enter them as events in Outlook on their "done by" date with a 3 day (or more or less) reminder. When the reminder comes up an email is sent or call is made to remind the person of their action item. Outlook's reminder is thus a structure to maintain the activities needed for the series of meetings.

Other actions which can use some help from structures could include assignments (or more gently phrased as requests) or promises that the person made to the meeting group.

In many cases the minutes of a meeting could consist mostly of actions like:

Date activity assigned	The actual request or promise	Person(s) who has agreed to this	Date promised or requested item to be done
3/7	Draft budget for discussion	Mary M.	3/15
2/28	Audit completion	John P.	3/11

In any case a reliable practice or system for follow-up and reminding people will, just by itself, improve the outcome from your meetings This structure will not improve meetings directly but it will dramatically improve meeting actions and outcomes. It will also improve morale since it is demotivating to sit in meetings where agreed-upon actions have not been handled.

You may have to manage action items hanging over from prior meetings.

Idea for action: Consider using a single list with additions for new items and deletions (or instead of deletion use a strike through font) for completed items.

Lesson 5
Great minutes preserve the accomplishments and decisions

Reference: Meeting Improvement Idea Book, Chapter 5

Some people call them minutes (especially for more formal meetings); others call them notes. Minutes are legal requirements of certain types of meetings. This includes public meetings for government agencies, board meetings for corporations and various other official types of meetings.

Bad memory effect: *Within 2 weeks of the meeting, most people will forget what was covered, decided and promised. The research shows that people's recollection of the meeting is between 50% and 90% wrong. Thus it is important to create and maintain accurate records of the collective decisions made in meetings.*

Minutes have three major functions for organizations:
- *Perhaps most importantly, they announce decisions made regarding the issues of importance to the organization. They inform the larger audience of what was decided by the group.*
- *Remind people of past decisions*
- *They remind people of what they agreed to do or what was assigned to them (usually) by the next meeting.*

They also serve several secondary functions, typically:
- *To provide an actual list of attendees*
- *To provide legal notice that the meeting took place*
- *To create a history of the organization*
- *Capture ideas for further refinement*
- *To describe the topics and issues discussed at a meeting*

- *To briefly list comments or discussions on those issues*

Idea for action: *Print the agenda with triple (or more) spacing for the secretary to take minutes on so all topics can be covered and there is space to write decisions and assignments. Even if notes are taken electronically, the spacing will help the note taker keep various sections of the meeting distinct from each other.*

As with most things, some prep work ahead of time will make the process simpler, quicker and more accurate. In addition to printing the agenda (with a lot of while space), print the attendee list so you can just check off people as they arrive, it may help to make a map of the seating arrangements. Some organizations print name tags and use the tags for attendance.

Ideas on the minutes themselves
- *Make notes during the meeting and write them up after the meeting – preferably within 48 hours.*
- *Generally don't describe all the "he said, she said" details. Record topics discussed, decisions made, and action items.*
- *Don't include information that will embarrass anyone unless it can't be avoided*
- *Do use positive language*
- *Consider an action item section in the minutes so people can easily see what is expected*
- *Whenever there are new people or guests attending, make sure to ask for contact information for the minutes*
- *Next meeting: When? Where? What topics to be covered? Why?*
- *Keep an archive of minutes, both recent and further back*

Lesson 6
How, why and when to use the Meeting Defender calculator

Have you ever sat in a meeting thinking that an awful lot of hours and real dollars were being wasted? People (probably even you!) sit in badly run meetings fidgeting, bored, daydreaming, texting friends and otherwise losing productive work time. The cost of all this wasted time is an important reason to get a handle on this time drain.

You can also consider the money spent as a stand-in for the effort put into that meeting. From that information you can determine if the investment is worth it.

We have created the Meeting Defender software calculator to help you track and analyze your meetings. Management gurus are quick to point out that what can't be measured can't be managed. This calculator makes meetings measurable in an easy to learn, easy to use application.

Meeting Defender can additionally be used to help you understand aspects of your meeting culture. It can help you answer questions like:

- *How long do our meetings average?*
- *How many people attend?*
- *Do people come and go during the meetings?*
- *How much money (direct dollars) do our meetings cost us?*
- *Do adopting new rules for meetings lead to more productive meetings?*

The major components of this software include:
- *Meeting Timer*
- *Meeting Cost Calculator*
- *Tracking attendance*

Information can be exported to Excel for storage and further analysis.

To use this software you will need to input the participants and their salaries or wages, or an estimate of them. But problem #1 is that salaries are confidential, and your guesses may not be very accurate. The simplest solution is to assign people into general categories such as operations, engineer, supervisor, vice president, etc. The calculation should also include the overhead costs of those hours using a multiplier for other costs. We use 2.2 for the overhead; your organization may differ. So to calculate the charge rate we would apply the multiplier times the average wage for that job equals the charge rate.

A $60,000 a year job would be about $30 an hour (assuming 2000 hours per year); multiplied by 2.2 equals $66 as a charge rate. A $100,000 a year job would be $50 an hour; multiplied by 2.2 equals $110 as a charge rate.

Assignment: *Start using Meeting Defender to measure the costs for each meeting. After each meeting, download the results into an Excel spread sheet.*

Lesson 7
Self-assessment of your meetings

By now both you and the team are probably more conscientious than you have ever been before about your meetings. Still there is more progress that can be made. So far we have concentrated on the outside envelope of the meeting; now it is time to delve into the inner workings of the meeting.

To do this we need to deal with the perceptions of the participants and some subjective reactions they may have. For example, you might think the purpose of the meeting is crystal clear. Quite possibly your participants do not share that view.

Beware of your reaction to (honest) feedback. Accept it or not, but do make a point of learning from it. Do not over-react, defend or argue about it. Instead, consider that others didn't understand it the same way you did, and think what you might do differently next time so that their take-away will end up closer to yours.

It is completely OK for you to think one thing and for them think something entirely different.

***Assignment:** Create and use a meeting assessment tool for participants to fill out after each meeting.*

Our standard assessment tool (adapt for your own purposes):

Area or antidote	Lesson to return to, discuss,read about, experiment with	Reference and review
A	Action item list and procedure	Lesson 3, Read Chapter 5
C	Checklist	Lesson 1, Read Chapter 7
F	Facilitation & facilitator	Read Chapters 8, 10
G	Ground Rules	Lesson 2, Read chapter 3
M	Minutes	Lesson 5, Read Chapter 5
N	Agenda	Lesson 4, Read Chapter 4
P	Participants	Read Chapters 3, 6

Survey Question	Area	Grade and Comments
Was the purpose of the meeting clear?	F	People rambled and the chair never brought them back to the point.
Did the setup of the room and logistics help or hinder the meeting process and could it be improved?	C	Maybe a table with chairs around it would be better than using an auditorium for just 9 people.
Were people reminded of their action items called everyone before the meeting?	A	Yes, the administrative assistant the day before.
Did the agenda reflect the true business of this group?	N	No agenda provided.
(add anything important to you) Etc		

Meeting Process

Survey Question	Area	Grade and Comments
Did the meeting follow the agenda?	N	
Did people come late, come and go, or l eave early without knowledge of the chair?	G, F, P	
Did the meeting start and end on time +5-10 minutes	G, F	
Did the group use conflict in a positive way to differentiate ideas?	F	
Did the group work toward consensus?	F, P	
Did the team leader intervene when the process seemed ineffective?	F	
Was facilitation even handed and effective? F Did the group insist on action commitments (what is to be done, by when and who)?	A, P	
How did you feel when you left the meeting (excited, sleepy, raring to get to work, headachy, etc.)?	All	
(add anything important to you)		

Afterwards and follow-up

Survey Question	Area	Grade and Comments
Was the action plan published and was it clear who was to do what by when?	A, M	
Did minutes come out in a short time after the meeting?	M	
Did they reflect what you remembered from the meeting?(add anything important to you)	M	

How to tabulate
- *Create a spreadsheet with all the questions down the left column.*
- *At the top of the spreadsheet put the date and meeting name*
- *Put the grade and comment across from the question and in line with the date.*
- *Average the grades for each survey question.*
- *Compare the average grades for each survey question as you continue to refine your meeting practice. Note changes in a positive and negative direction. Thus you can chart progress made in changing your meeting culture.*

Lesson 8
Using the assessment

To make sure no bias creeps in, someone other than the facilitator or even someone in an entirely different group should tabulate the surveys. They may be able to be more objective than a person who feels their own work is being measured and evaluated.

No matter what the results are, the information is useful feedback for both the facilitator and for the group.

Area or antidote	Lesson to return to, discuss, read about, experiment with	Reference and review
A	Action item list and procedure	Lesson 3, Read Chapter 5
C	Checklist	Lesson 1, Read Chapter 7
F	Facilitation and facilitator	Read Chapters 8, 10
G	Ground Rules	Lesson 2, Read chapter 3
M	Minutes	Lesson 5, Read Chapter 5
N	Agenda	Lesson 4, Read Chapter 4
P	Participants	Read Chapters 3, 6

How to use the information gained

If you want to get better at something, try setting up instant feedback. This lesson is designed to review the feedback and put it to work improving your meetings.

What if your feedback is that meetings exceed the length allotted? What could you do?

1   *Reduce the number of agenda items*
2   *Manage time better (keep a tighter hold on discussions, cut off repeated information)*
3   *Schedule a longer meeting*
4   *Manipulate the environment to speed up the meeting: Remove the coffee, donuts, chairs, make the room colder, etc.*
5   *Put times on each agenda item and appoint a time keeper.*
6   *Consider talking less and listening more.*

In every case the feedback can be used to positively impact the effectiveness of your meetings.

Pick the areas that need the most work for use in the last Lesson.

Lesson 9
Identifying the 7 symptoms
of bad meetings
and what to do about them

Various studies estimate that there are between 10 and 17 million meetings on an average day in the United States, or more than three billion meetings per year. A meeting between several managers or executives may cost upwards of $1000 per hour in salary costs alone.

All these meetings, and yet managers, supervisors, engineers and workers agree that many meetings are a waste of time. Do you ever get frustrated, getting called to attend meetings that seem to waste too much time? Do you ever wish you could do something about it?

Some symptoms to look for:

1. **Do certain meetings ramble on, lack a clear purpose, lack an agenda, have an agenda that nobody follows?**
   Good meeting practice says that a specific agenda will reduce the time wasted in a meeting. A poll of 471 management leaders noted that 90 percent of those polled attributed the failure of most meetings to a "lack of advanced planning and organization." Not only is an agenda important; empowering people to point out when the meeting goes off the agenda can be essential too. Review Chapters 1 and 4.

2. *Did you ever notice people doing their own thing during the meeting: texting, talking on the phone, responding to email, carrying on unrelated conversations.*

One way to avoid this: establish or review your ground rules before the meeting begins. Ground rules are the rules and regulations people agree on. Rules could include limits on texting, email and telephone conversations, no off-board conversations, etc. People may need to be reminded of the ground rules at the beginning of the meeting, or during the meeting's course. Review Chapter 3.

3. *Is it common that people are not prepared – they have not read the report, document, spread sheet that the meeting was about or have not done the research they promised?*

A well-run organization holds staff members accountable for doing their jobs and keeping their promises. People have roles in any organization, and frequently other people rely on them to do what they said or promised. Meetings are often places where people are expected to report on their work, share information, etc. When members fail to do what is expected of them, they waste other people's time who came to the meeting in order to learn what progress has been made. Holding people accountable could be part of the ground rules. Review Chapter 3.

4. *Are decisions discussed but not decided? When decisions are made, do people continue to fight them, disavow them or bad-mouth them afterwards?*

A good business process gets essential activities done with a minimum of waste. A good meeting process requires decisions or requires that the topic be continued to the next meeting. If a decision still can't be made, the decision may need to be kicked upstairs or assigned to a sub-group.

The second issue is that after everyone has had their say and decisions are made, the decision needs to be supported by the whole group, even if some disagree. Special exception: where the decision is illegal, immoral or dangerous. Review Chapter 3.

5. *Are your meetings dominated by a few talkers (not necessarily the leader)? Conversely, are there knowledgeable people who are never heard from?*

Facilitation can improve the process and outcome of meetings. If there is no one in the group who feels skilled enough to facilitate, you may consider bringing in an outsider to run a few meetings while the group continues to study the meeting process on their own. According to an article in the Fall 2006 issue of The Facilitator newsletter, using a skilled meeting facilitator can increase the productivity of a project by 25%. Of course they might have a bias, but having someone with training in meeting facilitation can improve most meetings. Review Chapters 8, 10.

6. *Do people come late, or come and go? Do meetings start late and end late?*

Integrity – consider the integrity of the steel beams in a building. If one or more was missing, wouldn't the building sag or fall down? The integrity of your work group or team is similarly undermined when key people are missing; it doesn't matter if this is from being late, leaving early, or failing to show up at all. They might miss important communications or waste everyone else's time when they have to be specially brought up to date. Review Chapter 3.

7. *Did you ever leave a meeting with a headache or excessively tired? Do you usually leave certain meetings angry, frustrated or depressed?*

Is your style of meeting healthy for people? Do you go in and sit down with donuts, coffee, soft drinks, bagels and other foods that spike your blood sugar and then cause it to crash? Are meetings longer than necessary or are they run without breaks? Are you holding the wrong type of meeting for any particular time of day? Consider the logistics of the meeting to see if your meetings actually help or hinder the work of the organization. Review Chapters 6 and   8.

Industry Week magazine estimates that meetings waste 37 billion dollars a year in the US alone. Some of that money is being wasted in your organization!

Lesson 10
Get more great ideas to
continue to improve

The Meeting Idea Book *has about a hundred ideas that can have a positive impact on your meetings. This should become an important reference for you, to keep turning to in order to keep improving.*

Have you been wondering how you will keep up the momentum of the process that you started 10 weeks ago? It would be all too easy to revert to your old ways since the new ways might not have become habits yet. Without some practices built into your meetings, the whole process might revert back to square one. The key is to keep looking at your meeting culture, meeting process and your meeting procedures.

How to keep the process alive

In Lesson 7 you spent a week filling out feedback forms about your meetings. These forms contain valuable steps to be climbed toward the next summit of your meeting process. In Lesson 8 you tallied the responses into a useful format. You also used your Meeting Defender Meeting Calculator to demonstrate some of the objective facts about your meetings.

First things first
- *Compare the Lesson 8 surveys to the original ones done at the very beginning of the process. Note what progress has been made (pat yourselves on the back). You might also look for such qualitative indicators as:*
- *People leave the meeting in a better mood*
- *Room logistics snafus reduced or eliminated*

- *Agenda being followed*
- *Action items being handled with less effort*
- *Compare any base line data developed by the initial usage of the Meeting Defender Meeting Calculator with the use of the calculator in Lesson 7. Note statistics for the same meeting. What do you see?*
- *Look for people staying in the meeting longer, coming and going less*
- *Meetings starting and ending on time. Some meetings may even be shorter than before, or the same length but with more work getting done*

Second step
- *Review the questionnaires and make a list of the areas that still need work.*
- *Each week or month, address each item with a self-designed simple 10 minute lesson (sometimes called a single point lesson).*
- *Try out material from the checklists in the Appendix to The Meeting Idea Book*
- *Continue until you run through all the items.*
- *For 1 week or month, run surveys for all the meetings.*
- *For 1 week or month, run Meeting Defender Meeting Calculator to gather objective data.*
- *Do "first things first" again.*
- *Repeat!*

THE MEETING IDEA BOOK

The Meeting Idea Book
Table of Contents

Chapter 1

Some background about meetings

This work about meetings has grown out of consulting and training assignments I have undertaken around the world over the last 30 years. What I began to see was that it didn't matter if an organization was a world leader in industry, a governmental agency or a small family business; across all these types of enterprises there were great gaps between organizations with "good" meeting practices and organizations with "bad" ones. And since meetings play such a big part of life in organizations, the quality of meetings makes a huge difference in the efficiency of organizations and the satisfaction of workers and management as well.

If you are in one of the good organizations, consider yourself lucky. Undoubtedly you enjoy your job more than most of the rest of the working world, and your ability to contribute has been dramatically increased because of the greatly improved communications among different groups at work.

If you are not in one of the better meetings organizations, I am sorry. But you are holding in your hand some strong medicine to cure the very condition we have just diagnosed.

Are your meetings a joke?

Meetings in the news:

April 1, 2010 *Washington, DC*

In recognition of the importance of meetings in business, government, schools, churches, teams, clubs and other aspects of public life, today has been designated National Meeting Day in the United States and other participating countries (check with your local event calendar).

To celebrate this vital institution, every citizen is encouraged to host or attend a meeting, be it live or online, or to simply watch C-SPAN all day.

Traditional Meeting Day menus include coffee and doughnuts, assorted sandwiches and cold delivery pizza. It is also appropriate to offer customers and employees gifts of pens, tee shirts and mugs imprinted with business logos to commemorate the day.

November 16, 2012, *Johannesburg, South Africa*

When his wife went into early labor, Armond Beary was on a business trip – in South Africa. With no way to get home in time, he turned to GoToMeeting to enable him to share in this special event.

"Since we hosted our wedding using GoToWebinar,* I knew GoToMeeting would be the perfect solution for me to use at the birth of our first child," says Beary. "It was great! I sent my assistant to the hospital with a laptop, and before you know it I was going over our PowerPoint labor plan with my wife, the doctor and the nurses just as if I were there …"

For Immediate Release, *San Francisco, CA*

Meeting Czar Inc., a Silicon Valley start-up, has developed a new Bluetooth presenter with green and red laser pointer, full PowerPoint and multimedia control and exclusively, a water pistol accurate up to 15 feet (5 meters) ...

Meetings Are Another Way To Avoid WORK!

Are you making decissions all by yourself?

Are you annoyed with taking on all the responsibility?

HOLD A MEETING!!!

- **You can mingle with the staff**
- **Collaborate on ideas**
- **Feel important**
- **Show off**
- **Impress the higer ups**
- **Serve coffee and cake**

All On Your Boss's Dime!!!

Adapted from the blog of Richard Richmeyer

Meetings are the butt of jokes because everyone in business suffers some amount of distress about them. Nevertheless, the second there is an issue which needs discussion, a meeting will be called, because it is the simplest way to gather all the parties together who need to weigh in on the issues at hand. Meetings are addictive but there are no meetings for people to admit they are meeting addicts!

Meetings: the good and the bad

One of the most important aspects of meetings is the human aspect. We are wired to be social beings and to work and play with other human beings. Don't discount the importance of this. No matter how badly the meeting is run, there is enormous value for human beings to meet together and work toward a common goal.

If you work with others, knowing (and at least minimally trusting) them can be a benefit. That is why some socializing before and after meetings is important. Even the fishing conversations, says Andrew Levitt, a project manager in the energy industry, are useful as long as they are reigned in.

Model for value

People in groups have a powerful effect on each other. These powerful effects could be viewed as a spectrum from the sublime to the ridiculous or even the dangerous. Good meetings can reflect one end of the spectrum; bad meetings can demonstrate the other.

The sublime outcome results when people add their knowledge and experience together to build an outcome that any single one of them would have been unable build. Frequently the results are so much better that synergy is created. That is the 1+1+1 equals 5 effect, where the outcome of the group is significantly better than the work output of each of the individuals by themselves. This could be the goal of all our meetings – greatly enhanced productivity and the satisfaction of time well spent.

We are all too familiar with the other end of the spectrum. Truly bad meetings can span from the ridiculous (including mind numbing boredom, having to listen to pontification, excessive pointless arguing and general time wasting) to the gatherings which result in negative productivity and destructive behavior (examples: dangerous witch hunts and mob behaviors – yes, this can happen even within polite professional organizations).

The pain of meetings: bad meetings stifle everyone

In an ideal world, all meetings would be effective ones: concise, pleasant, creators of new ideas or consensus for how the group should move ahead. Sam Parker (co-founder of Givemore.com, a company that publishes useful messages and ideas for meeting communications) describes his vision:

"A meeting should make all attendees better; each person should leave with something he/she didn't have before. That could be some new knowledge about a product or initiative. It could be a new skill after a training seminar. It could even be inspiration or a better attitude that helps the person do his or her job better."

Yet all too often there is a gap between what a meeting could or should be and what it actually feels like to most of the people forced to endure it.

I often ask people in my seminars around the world to raise their hands if the meetings they attend are a pain in the neck. (I am not always quite that polite in my choice of language, but you probably get the idea.) Almost every hand shoots up. All across the world meetings come up as the biggest waste of leadership and worker time, bar none.

Is this true for you? Research conducted by the Annenberg School of Communications at UCLA and the University of Minnesota's Training & Development Research Center show that executives on average spend 40-50% of their working hours in meetings. That's half their workday used up in meetings. These studies also point out that as much as 50% of meeting time is unproductive and that up to 25% is spent discussing irrelevant issues.

Let's imagine a typical day in a major organization. A meeting has been called for several members of a department. According to a survey by MCI Conferencing (now part of Verizon), most professionals admit to one or more of the following transgressions:

- (91%) Daydreaming
- (96%) Missing meetings
- (95%) Missing parts of meetings
- (73%) Bringing other work to meetings
- (39%) Dozing off during meetings.

The problem is that such meeting inefficiencies affect you and your organization as well. Some direct effects of unproductive meetings include:

- Meetings are longer than they need to be, less efficient and generating fewer results
- More meetings are needed to accomplish the same objectives
- With so much time wasted in ineffective meetings, employees have less time to get their own work done
- Ineffective meetings create frustration at all staff levels
- Information generated in unproductive meetings often isn't managed properly
- Inefficient meetings cost organizations billions of dollars each year in otherwise productive employee work time

Why on earth would smart managers allow this situation to continue?

- Most individuals have never experienced or witnessed the power of a truly effective meeting (have you?) and therefore don't recognize how bad their meetings are.
- Even if they have experienced (or even run) a great meeting, they do not understand enough of effective meeting dynamics to replicate their previous success.
- People resist changing the way things have always been done.

- People feel they do not have the time, resources or understanding of how to improve their meetings.
- There is something seductive in running the meeting "your way." This might be even truer when your way doesn't work well.
- What's the big deal, people sometimes say. Why does it matter if we waste a little time, this once? (Yet ask yourself, is it ever just this once?)

Marc Archambault, a leading meeting trainer, suggests that people hate meetings for a variety of reasons. Sometimes the participants do not sense a clear purpose; sometimes they may lack structure or a visible agenda. Sometimes the group gathers in uncomfortable rooms. People complain of awkward conversations with the same few people blathering on; people don't listen to each other in a respectful manner, and so on. The bottom line is that the meetings don't actually accomplish anything, and they can even move an organization backwards.

GiveMore.com, a management consulting firm, spent a week in 2011 asking people to take a one-question survey. Their question: "What frustrates you most about meetings at work?"

More than 1600 people sent in answers. The outpouring of responses supported the above observations. The 10 most common responses:

- Allowing attendees to ramble and repeat the same comments or thoughts
- Doesn't start on time, stay on track, or finish on time
- No specific action items or walk-away points
- No clear purpose or objective
- Not inspiring or motivating
- Not organized or no agenda
- Too long

- Repeating information for late arrivals
- Weak presenter (unprepared, monotone, overly redundant)
- Meetings are boring with nothing new or interesting presented

The loss of money, time and energy is not the worst part of bad meetings!

The worst cost is more personal. It is your energy, your enthusiasm, your feelings of satisfaction that are sacrificed by frequent, bad meetings. Think of a bad meeting not as an inconvenience (which it is), but as a theft of energy, thus robbing you and your colleagues, and diminishing the contribution each might make to the organization as a whole.

The satisfaction for many of us comes from making a contribution. Bad meetings stifle everyone by draining the enthusiasm, the energy, the motivation for working above and beyond the barest minimum needed to get by.

These losses can actually be measured, or at least estimated. We can use time and money burned (as used in the Meeting Defender software discussed later) as proxies or stand-ins for other losses from bad meetings that are harder to measure. Once we have something to measure, we can monitor any progress made. If we can cut down the time spent to run certain meetings while still getting the same work done, then perhaps we have improved our meeting culture (and maybe our whole work lives).

7 symptoms of bad meetings and what to do about them

Bad meetings may differ from each other. But they often share some common characteristics. Some symptoms to look for:

1. Do certain meetings ramble on, lack a clear purpose, lack an agenda, or have an agenda that nobody follows?

Good meeting practice says that a specific agenda will almost always reduce the time wasted in a meeting (discussed in greater depth in Chapter 4). A poll of 471 management leaders noted that 90 percent of those polled attributed the failure of most meetings to a lack of advanced planning and organization. Not only is an agenda important; empowering people to point out when the meeting veers off the agenda can be useful too.

2. Do you ever notice people doing their own thing during the meeting: texting, talking on the phone, responding to email, carrying on unrelated conversations?

One way to avoid this: establish some ground rules that everyone agrees on before the meeting begins. These rules could include removing temptations by setting limits on texting, email and telephone conversations, no off-board conversations, requiring people to listen without interrupting, etc.

Even if people have agreed in advance to these rules, they may need to be reminded of the ground rules at the beginning of the meeting, or during the meeting's course (for particularly egregious ground rule breaking). Such reminding may be done by fellow members or by the meeting leader, if there is one.

3. Do people show up who are not prepared – who have not read the report, document or spread sheet that the meeting was about or have not done the research they promised?

Holding people accountable should be part of any set of ground rules. A well-run organization holds staff members accountable for doing their jobs and keeping their promises. People have roles to play in any organization, and other people rely on them to do what they said or promised, in order to build on that foundation. Meetings are places where people report on their work, share information, etc. When members fail to do what they promised, they are being disrespectful of other people's time who came to the meeting in order to participate or learn what progress has been made. This creates actual economic waste of organizational resources, as well as being rude to coworkers.

4. Is there closure for decision making? Are decisions discussed but not decided? Is there agreement to support collective decisions once they are made? When decisions are made, do people continue to fight them, disavow them or bad-mouth them afterwards?

A good business process gets essential activities done with a minimum of waste. A good meeting process requires decisions or a decision that the topic be continued to the next meeting. If a decision still can't be made, the decision may need to be kicked upstairs or assigned to a sub-group.

Then, after everyone has had their say and decisions are made, the decision needs to be supported by the entire group, even if some disagree. Otherwise the disagreements move underground and undermine the workings of all.

Special exception: where the decision is illegal, immoral or dangerous. In such cases, dissent may be healthier for the organization in the long run than cooperation in the short run with bad decisions.

5. Are your meetings dominated by a few talkers (not necessarily the leader)? Conversely, are there knowledge

able people who never volunteer to speak up?

Facilitation can improve both the process and the outcome of meetings. According to an article in the Fall 2006 issue of *The Facilitator,* using a skilled meeting facilitator increases the productivity of a project by 25%. Of course the magazine may have a bias, but having someone with training in meeting facilitation has the potential to improve most meetings.

6. Do people come late, or leave before the end? Do meetings start and end late?

Timeliness is a matter of integrity. Here we are using the word "integrity" in the sense of being unimpaired or sound. Consider the integrity of the steel beams in a building. If one or more was missing or askew, wouldn't the building sag or fall down? Similarly, the integrity of your work group or team is undermined when key people are missing during updates or decision-making times; it doesn't matter why or how. They will inevitably miss important communications, updates, reframing of the issues under discussion, and waste everyone else's time when they have to be specially brought up to date. Because they missed the original sequence of events, they may also leave the meeting with an erroneous impression of what was discussed or agreed upon.

7. Did you ever leave a meeting with a headache or excessively tired? Do you leave certain meetings angry, frustrated or depressed?

Is your current style meeting healthy for you? Do you go in and sit down with donuts, coffee, soft drinks, bagels and other foods that spike your blood sugar and then cause it to crash? Are meetings longer than necessary or are they run without breaks? Are you holding the wrong type of meeting for the particular time of day? Consider the logistics of the meeting to see if your meetings actually help or hinder the work of the organization.

Industry Week estimates that meetings waste $37 billion a year in the US alone. Some of that money may have been wasted in your own organization!

What is strange about this situation is that it isn't on the top of anyone's list to get fixed. If we are wasting billions, why don't corporations make the effort to fix the problem? Sam Parker, GiveMore's co-founder, made an interesting comment. "What's most interesting is that all of these are controllable and cost no money," he said. "So why aren't people fixing these things? I think it goes back to a lack of peer-to-peer accountability."

Why have meetings if they are the source of so many complaints?

As Winston Churchill once said about democracy, it's the worst possible system ... except for all the others. Consider these alternatives to having a meeting:

- Phone – a good way to exchange information, except that many folks do not answer their phone when you want them to. Sometimes conference calls work well (some would just call them meetings by another name) but they introduce their own unique set of problems.
- Email – another way to exchange information, except that it can be hard to get people's attention, some will not read beyond the first paragraph or so, and it is difficult to get the correct read on the person's tone. Most of all, it is difficult to secure any committed action from an email request.

- Print and distribute – another tried and true way to communicate, except for the amount of extra work to write up all the issues, and the lack of collaboration that goes into the product. It does have the virtue that reading flyers or other printed summaries can stimulate people to think.

So we keep on having meetings...

Why? The answer is simple, **no one has thought of a better way to get business done**. In most organizations, good and effective meetings are the kick-starter for action. Without meetings and the communications and agreement they can generate, no action takes place.

If meetings are the poison, here are some antidotes:

- Figure out just how bad the situation is. Analysis and measurement are the first steps towards solving most difficult situations. For one month, track all meetings for your work group. You may use various tools to gather information: notes, questionnaires to evaluate subjective information, and your Meeting Defender Meeting Calculator (described in a later chapter) for objective information tallying up the time and costs spent in your meetings. Use the facts generated by these tools to demonstrate the problem, drive the improvement, and measure the gains as you continue to make improvements in how your organization's meetings are conducted. See Chapter 12 for more ideas.
- Get your people trained. There are many books, seminars and workshops available to educate people on running better meetings. Three major areas to focus on: facilitation, meeting etiquette and being a good team member.
- Find out and use new technologies. Technologies range from computer-linked white boards that download or print

meeting notes and agreements, to on-line meeting software. Several applications in collaboration technology
focus on improving efficiency by reducing the steps to go
from the beginning of collaboration to final products.

- After evaluation, after training and after new technology is
adopted, retest your meetings using Meeting Defender and
your questionnaires to demonstrate how far you've come.
Additional details can be found in Chapter 13.

Writer Eric Matson described one corporation's approach to
ensuring better meetings:

- Intel Corporation is an example of an organization that
takes its meetings very seriously. Walk into any conference
room at any Intel factory or office anywhere in the world
and you will see a poster on the wall with a series of simple
questions about the meetings that take place there: Do you
know the purpose of this meeting? Do you have an agenda? Do you know your role? Every new employee, from
the most junior production worker to the highest ranking
executive, is required to take the company's course on
effective meetings. For years, the course was taught by
CEO Andy Grove, who believed that good meetings were
such an important part of Intel's culture that it was worth
his time to train all employees. "In our training program,
we talk a lot about meeting discipline," says Michael Fors,
corporate training manager at Intel University. "It isn't
complicated. It's doing the basics well: structured agendas,
clear goals, paths that you're going to follow. These things
make a huge difference."

See the appendix for an example.

George David Kieffer, in his book, *The Strategy of Meetings*, notes, "I decided to talk with some of America's most successful and respected leaders in business, labor, industry, education and government – many of whom are viewed as masters in the art of conducting meetings. In speaking with over fifty of those leaders, two central points emerged. Number one, the skill to manage a meeting – to develop ideas, to motivate people and to move people and ideas to positive action – is perhaps the most critical asset in any career. And number two, most professionals have had no real training in devising and managing an effective meeting; in fact, most professionals do not recognize the enormous impact their meetings have on their organizations and their careers."

Idea for action: *Look up and attend training opportunities for improving your meetings. You and your coworkers could even attend different trainings and compare notes.*

Leverage – Huge opportunity for improved effectiveness

Training in better meetings = more productivity for each member of the team. That is the very definition of leverage, where a few small changes can have a greatly magnified effect. Unfortunately the opposite is also true. Bad meetings make for lost productivity for the whole work group (the leverage working in the opposite direction).

An executive in 5 hours of meetings a day has a direct impact on perhaps 20 people and indirect impact on an additional 100, depending on his or her position in the organization. A supervisor on the factory floor may have a leveraged impact of 1:10 (called the span of control).

Consider the effect of off-topic discussions, where attention at the meeting drifts away from the common business at hand. The 20 minute discussion about fishing or politics (however important those topics are) just cost your team four hours because 12 people in attendance each had that third of an hour wasted. Four hours lost due to a short conversation! You and the staff could have been working on that marketing plan, engineering a new product, helping craftspeople with supply problems, planning the next wave of jobs or even completing the odds and ends of tasks so you could have a clean desk.

Some may argue that a little bit of socializing is crucial to establishing the bonds that allow cooperation between people in organizations. This is also true. Like many things, there are costs and benefits to be balanced before an ever-shifting optimum can be achieved. A mindful meeting participant intuitively understands the principal of leverage and acts accordingly. Social moments should be conducted while people are waiting for the meeting to begin, in smaller groups at breaks or at the end of the meeting, or limited to short jokes or anecdotes during the meeting as necessary for the purpose of illustrating a point, alleviating tension, or moving the group onto the next topic for discussion.

These limitations are important because of the high cost of that leveraged time. While the actual cost of the 4 hours lost (returning to the example above) is tough to calculate, it can be substantial. Each of those 12 people will have a different pay rate, and their level of benefits and the overhead costs of their time are even more complex to calculate. Yet those are real costs, both to the organization and to the levels of enthusiasm and commitment of the individuals involved. On the other hand, any cost savings from avoiding that loss are also tough to determine. While the savings might not show up in in the General Ledger, they will result indirectly in higher productivity, higher morale, lower turnover and greater serenity among the staff.

A University of Arizona study on teamwork estimated there

are more than 11 million formal meetings per day in the United States - more than three billion meetings per year. They found that managers spend about 20% of their time in formal meetings of 5 people or more. A meeting between several managers or executives may cost upwards of $1000 per hour in salary costs alone. A Fortune 50 company estimates losses in excess of $75 million per year due to poor meeting procedures.

Russell L. Kratowicz, editor of Plant Services, says, "Meetings are expensive. Put 10 people in a conference room for four hours and you'll burn up no less than $1,200 in direct wages alone. Add benefits and a lunch, and the cost rises to $1,500 Repeat this routine twice a week, and you'll spend more than $150,000 a year. Top it off with the value-add of the useful work these people were unable to perform because of the meetings and the grand total is anybody's guess."

Meeting Defender software can calculate the direct cost of any meeting and make it available for your discussions about meeting improvement. The indirect costs you will have to guess at. Some use a standard multiplier – say 2 or more times the direct costs, depending on your industry or situation.

Meetings are a fact of life. After all, no matter what kind of work you do, you will have to meet with others at some time or another. In almost any line of work, indeed even while volunteering or pursuing family interests, meetings are a frequent necessity. We have a lot of meetings. And since we have so many, we may as well get good at them. Training to run or even attend meetings should be part of everyone's learning process. Getting good at life in groups will be an effort that will pay off for a lifetime. Yet when I poll my students from classes taught around the world as to how many have had a class on meeting etiquette, very few hands go up. Even in the nation's top business schools there is little training in this important yet basic skill.

These essential skills – running meetings and being a good team member – should be taught in any school that purports to train people for business. Perhaps they should even be part of the basic high school or grade school curriculum. We are social animals, we humans, and meeting with each other is part of how we conduct the business of life.

Some of the best organizations in the world offer training, guidelines and support to ensure good meeting etiquette. This may even be part of what allows them to become leaders in whatever line of work they pursue. If you are lucky, you've already learned how to run meetings from such a class or an expert. More commonly, the way most people learn about meetings is to attend them. This often results in learning more about how to whine and complain to sympathetic coworkers than learning how to move a group forward together. Unfortunately most of us learn about meetings from untrained people who are simply muddling through. This book offers help to get you beyond the merely muddling point.

Enlivening or a bore?

Meetings can either be a dreaded bureaucratic ritual or a time to gather together and get some work done. While few people equate meetings with serious work, the reality is that you can actually achieve a lot during a meeting if you take the time to establish a cordial relationship with your fellow meeting mates. A good meeting may be a place to learn new information, create agreement about what people should be doing, assess progress, create recognition (and thus incentives) for good work done, a place to remove obstacles and resistance by agreeing on commonly held values or vision, etc. These things are all important; indeed they may be crucial to the on-going existence of the organization.

Decision Point: *Is this meeting actually necessary?*

Apart from all the good points about meetings, one of the most efficient ways to improve meetings is to not hold one in the first place!

If there is a better way to deal with an issue or cover a body of material, you may want to simply skip the meeting. Sometimes a conference call is more efficient because it reduces travel time. Other times an email can cover the issues. If there is no point or goal for the meeting, delay gathering people together until there is a need for it!

Good reasons for delay:

If you decide to have the meeting, scheduling conflicts should be seriously considered in deciding whether to have this meeting right now. Don't hold a meeting when key people won't be there; the absent decision maker might require you to revisit the issues all over again.

Unless the topic is an emergency, don't hold the meeting until all the preparation work can be completed. That would include an agenda, support materials and requests to read or research the issues under consideration.

Okechukwu, a Nigerian business humorist and motivational speaker, advocates for "No Meeting Mondays" (crafted after casual Fridays). People need time to work when they are free from time-consuming meetings. He advocates spending time and money training the staff in how to avoid having meetings.

Some of his more radical and humorous ideas include imposing a meeting tax when someone exceeds their meeting quota, or imprisonment for unauthorized meetings. He has a theory that the number of meetings expand as the number of meeting rooms expands. Perhaps by doing something else with those pesky conference rooms we could cut back on our meetings.

Underneath his humor is a reality that strikes many people as true. Meetings can be a horrible waste of time and resources. The productivity lost due to poor meeting practices should be the concern of management.

The art of managing meetings

Managing meetings is a highly skilled art form including three different areas of focus:

Establishing and maintaining good meeting practices: When you join an organization, there is already a meeting culture and ground rules in play. This culture is like the air in the room and it is invisible and present even if no one explicitly discusses how to run meetings. Our position is that the culture and the ground rules can be changed to make your meetings work better. These include facilitation, ground rules, and specific systems followed. Practices include respect for others, tools (Meeting Defender, timers, gavel, etc.) and meeting etiquette.

Agenda and subject matter: The agenda is the road map for the meeting. The subject matter is the purpose or reason for the meeting in the first place. Without a reason for the meeting, the meeting will meander (but you might not even notice if there is no agenda).

Follow-up and accountability: Follow-up is one of the toughest problems to manage in business. People promise to do a task and then they may consciously or unconsciously forget. There is an art to follow-up without resorting to punitive action.

Holding people accountable for what they promise or what you've requested is important to the smooth functioning of the whole work group. Many people avoid accountability measures, often because of previous experiences where accountability measures were used to punish or blame. However in a system that holds people accountable for their promises and actions without inappropriate punishments, accountability measures are more a reminder system, allowing greater reliability and trust to develop. Once people experience an accountability system without blame, they may find that their career development is linked to the accountability that they take on.

We will discuss each of these aspects of meeting management at greater length in the following chapters.

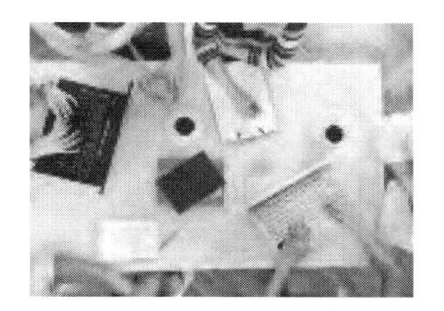

Chapter 2

Types of meetings

Many meetings encompass a variety of topics, and can be handled in many possible formats. Other kinds of meetings may require special formats to best accomplish what the organization needs from them. Types of meetings include:

- Legally required meetings (examples: board meetings, administrative hearings)
- Problem solving meetings whose agenda is restricted to the problem
- Investigations
- Meetings meant to motivate and inspire people
- Meetings to update or manage projects
- Social meetings for a variety of reasons and causes

Special considerations of these types of meetings may revolve around their greater or lesser need for formality.

In addition to formal, informal and special purpose meetings, we should consider scheduled and ad hoc (spontaneous) meetings. Each of these has pitfalls and opportunities.

Long-standing meetings

Sometimes a regularly scheduled meeting has outlived its usefulness and should be eliminated. In other cases the meeting is anachronistic (follows obsolete rules for no current reason). Following the example of zero-based budgeting, where every year each budget item must be justified in order to keep its place in the budget, an organization might choose to adopt a zero-based meeting budget where every standing meeting has to justify itself each year or vanish from existance.

Idea for action: *Every meeting has to be justified annually in the "Annual Zero-Based Meeting Justification."*

Chain of command and cooperation

One important distinction coming from the military is the term "chain of command." If the participants are in the meeting chair's chain of command, it is quite a bit easier to get people to cooperate and follow through on their promises. If the people are all peers in the same organization, social constraints may be enough to get people to cooperate and (at least minimally) follow up. Or they may not.

Cooperation may become a big issue in organizations where there is no designated leader. The consequences for not cooperating or not following up on promises are weaker, and thus group activities are more difficult to manage. In those cases an agreement on the meeting's ground rules is essential for success. Agreement as to the mission and desired outcomes also become more important.

The final special issue is a volunteer-staffed meeting. These meetings run thousands of large and small associations, non-profits, fraternal, artistic, religious, and educational organizations. For meetings in these organizations, some efficiency might have to be sacrificed to make sure the volunteers have a positive experience. If volunteers don't have a positive experience, they may not return, and the organization loses not only their participation but also any continuity in pursuing its objectives.

Formal Meetings

Some meetings are required by law to follow particular formats, and thus stick to the formalities set down by legislative or administrative fiat. Formal meetings usually result from some legal requirement (required by statute or by the bylaws of the organization). Formal meeting types span from the corporate board meeting (such as Exxon or Apple) to public hearings of governmental agencies (utility companies, school boards) to the deliberations of an elected body (Congress). Formal meetings are generally run according to their own historic rules, customs and traditions, but they may also conform to the formal set of rules established and published more than 100 years ago called Robert's Rules of Order.

Written by Henry Martyn Robert (May 2, 1837 – May 11, 1923) as the *Pocket Manual of Rules of Order for Deliberative Assemblies* (1876, SC Griggs, Chicago, IL). Robert, a lifelong engineer, was a Brigadier General in the U. S. Army Corps of Engineers and President of the Board of Engineers. His *Rules* were a collection of parliamentary rules modeled on those used at the time in the U. S. House of Representatives. According to the story, he wrote the manual in response to his own poor performance in leading a church meeting. He decided to improve by learning about parliamentary procedure before participating in any more meetings.

Robert's Rules have been adopted by organizations around the world as a way to maintain orderly discussion and minimize acrimony among meeting participants. To this day the set of rules he devised are maintained and updated by the Roberts Rules of Order Association.

In Robert's own words, "It is the fundamental right and obligation of deliberative assemblies to require all questions to be thoroughly discussed before taking action!" Discussion takes place through orderly processes as defined by his rules. No discussion or protest against a motion implies consent to the action proposed. Once action is taken, whatever decision is made will be carried out and binding on those voting and those they represent.

Some key guidelines from Robert's Rules:
1   A participant can obtain the floor (the right to speak) by being the first to stand when the person speaking has finished, then stating, "Mr./Madam Chairman." The participant must be recognized by the Chair before speaking. Raising your hand means nothing. Standing while another has the floor is out of order.
2   Debate cannot begin until the Chair has stated the motion or resolution and asked, "Are you ready for the question?" If no one rises, the chair calls for the vote.
3   Before the motion is stated by the Chair, members may suggest modification of the motion. The mover can modify as he/she pleases, or even withdraw the motion without consent of the seconder. If mover modifies, the seconder can withdraw the second.
4   The "immediately pending question" is the last question stated by the Chair.
5   The member moving the "immediately pending question" is entitled to preference on the floor.
6   No member can speak twice to the same issue until everyone else wishing to speak has spoken to it once.

7 All remarks must be directed to the Chair. Remarks must be courteous in language and deportment. This means avoiding personal issues, never alluding to others by name, never referring to their motives.

8 The agenda and all committee reports are merely recommended starting points. When presented to the assembly and a question is stated, debate begins and changes may be made.

Rules and procedures:

- Robert's Rules call for 4 types of motions: Main Motion, Subsidiary Motion, Privileged Motion and Incidental Motion.
- Point of Privilege: Pertains to noise, personal comfort, etc. – a participant should interrupt only if necessary.
- Parliamentary Inquiry: Inquire as to the correct motion - to accomplish a desired result, or raise a point of order.
- Point of Information: Generally applies to information desired from the speaker: "I should like to ask the speaker a question."
- Orders of the Day (Agenda): A call to adhere to the agenda (a deviation from the agenda requires suspending the rules).
- Point of Order: Infraction of the rules, or improper decorum in speaking. Must be raised immediately after the error is made.
- Main Motion: Brings new business (the next item on the agenda) before the assembly
- Divide the Question: Divides a motion into two or more separate motions (each must be able to stand on their own)
- Consider by Paragraph: Adoption of a paper is held until all paragraphs are debated and amended and the entire

paper is satisfactory. After all paragraphs are considered, the entire paper is then open to amendment, and paragraphs may be further amended. Any Preamble cannot be considered until debate on the body of the paper has ceased.

- Amend: Inserting or striking out words or paragraphs, or substituting whole paragraphs or resolutions.
- Withdraw/Modify Motion: Applies only after question is stated; the mover can accept an amendment without obtaining the floor.
- Commit/Refer/Recommit to Committee: State the committee to receive the question or resolution; if no committee exists, include size of committee desired and the method of selecting the members (by election or appointment).
- Extend Debate: Applies only to the immediately pending question; extends until a certain time or for a certain period of time.
- Limit Debate: Closing debate at a certain time or limiting to a certain period of time.
- Postpone to a Certain Time: State the time the motion or agenda item will be resumed.
- Object to Consideration: Objection must be stated before discussion or another motion is stated.
- Lay on the Table: Temporarily suspends further consideration/action on pending question; may be made after motion to close debate has carried or is pending.
- Take from the Table: Resumes consideration of item previously "laid on the table" - state the motion to take from the table.
- Reconsider: Can be made only by one on the prevailing side who has changed their position or view.
- Postpone Indefinitely: Kills the question/resolution for

this session. One exception: the motion to reconsider can be made during the same session.

- Previous Question: Closes debate if successful - may be moved to "Close Debate" if preferred.
- Informal Consideration: Move that the assembly go into "Committee of the Whole" – an informal debate as if in committee; this committee may limit number or length of speeches or close debate by other means by a 2/3 vote. All votes, however, are formal.
- Appeal Decision of the Chair: Appeal for the assembly to decide - must be made before other business is resumed; NOT debatable if relates to decorum, violation of rules or order of business.
- Suspend the Rules: Allows a violation of the assembly's own rules (except the Constitution); the object of the suspension must be specified.

Idea for action: *If you are involved in formal meetings, legally required meetings or public hearings, get a current copy of Robert's Rules of Order and read it.*

Neil Payne (author of "Business Meeting Etiquette") wrote some useful guidelines for formal meetings. These may seem somewhat anachronistic but are still followed in some places. He stresses that the underlying principles of business meeting etiquette are good manners, courtesy and consideration. If these principles are adhered to, the chances of being offensive and creating misunderstandings are greatly reduced.

He writes, "The business etiquette of formal meetings such as departmental meetings, management meetings, board meetings, negotiations and the like can be puzzling. Such meetings usually have a set format. For example, the chair may always be the same person; minutes, agendas or reports may be pre-distributed or voting may take place." Some key points include:

- Dress well and arrive in good time.
- If there is an established seating pattern, accept it. If you are unsure, ask.
- Acknowledge any introductions or opening remarks with a brief recognition of the chair and other participants.
- When discussions are under way, it is good business etiquette to allow more senior figures to contribute first.
- Never interrupt anyone, even if you disagree strongly. Note what has been said and return to it later with the chair's permission.
- Always address the chair unless it is clear that others are not doing so.
- It is a serious breach of business etiquette to divulge information to others about a meeting. What has been discussed should be considered as confidential.

Electronic meetings

One form that is increasingly popular is the teleconference meeting. Web based and telephone based meetings are a boon to large, multi-site organizations and projects. They can be a life saver when major components of an activity are being designed in one place, marketed in another and produced in a third place. Internet meetings follow most of the same principals of leverage as face to face meetings because the Internet meeting can really waste a lot of people's time at once.

There are several popular electronic meeting formats. At the low end is the simple telephone conference call (such as is available at freeconference.com). At the high end is the video conference from a purpose designed video conference room.

In between are Skype (and other) Internet based video conferences, Webconnect or GoToMeeting services. The older, operator-assisted conference calls still exist. Many of the conference calls (particularly the larger ones) are transmit only, with text questions directed to a moderator. But there are still increasing numbers of virtual meetings every year.

While in most cases the rules for a teleconference meeting are the same as an in-person meeting, there are some expansions for the different format.

- When you are announcing the meeting, be particularly clear about the time zone, call-in number and the pass-code to be used.
- Be clear about the timing. Be clear that the start time will be on time and not a few minutes later.
- If it is a hybrid Internet/telephone or Internet-only meeting, have a back-up plan in place for people who have technical problems and can't connect to the conference.
- If appropriate and available, record the meeting so late comers or no-shows can listen afterwards.
- For a teleconference, people should know how to control their phones (including such features as *6 to mute and unmute).
- If you are not speaking, you should be on mute.
- Have some ground rules regarding what people should do if they are interrupted. You can expect they will be interrupted (especially if they are at their desks).
- Take roll of the attendees first, so you and everyone else know who is there.
- As in a live meeting, any guests should introduce themselves and explain their role.

- When people talk, they should speak more clearly and slowly than normal and preface their contribution by stating their names.
- If there is to be a discussion, people should learn to pause and listen before going on.
- It is recommended that people spell out complex terms or show it on the screen (if available).
- Direct all questions and comments to specific individuals.
- Following the rules of etiquette is even more important than in live meetings.

Project meetings

Whenever you have a group of people involved in a common project, meetings become a key way to organize and manage progress. Project meetings loom large at the beginning of most projects and are designed to get people up to speed, solicit input, solve problems, and make sure nothing is forgotten. As the project progresses, the meetings often get smaller, requiring only the people immediately involved, and are more focused on particular issues relevant at that stage of the project.

In general it is better to have two short meetings per week rather than one long one. Shorter projects may have daily project meetings, but even long projects need frequent updates and communications. Short meetings tend to be more efficient for many reasons. Usually meetings start with a high energy and with a particular intention (to solve a problem, communicate a plan, etc.). After an hour people's minds start to wander and their focus erodes unless the meeting is managed very closely. Sometimes a quick 15-minute stand-up meeting is all that is needed. Don't let a 15 minute meeting become a 90 minute meander!

More frequent meetings are also useful in terms of overall project efficiency. The key to keeping projects on track is to detect problems early enough in the process that an intervention can be made before it is too late. It is no good finding out at a weekly meeting that an eight-day project is only half complete.

The beginning of a project is a good time to consider and organize not only the frequency of meetings but also the variety of types of meetings needed. In Turnaround Management, Tom Lenahan lists some of the meetings necessary to organize a shut-down of a factory, power plant or refinery to perform necessary maintenance. The series of meetings will typically include a Policy Team Meeting (meeting of the bosses), General Work-list Meeting, Major Task Review Meeting, Project Review Meeting, Inspection Review Meeting, Spare Parts Review Meeting, Plant Shutdown and Start-up Meeting, Safety Meeting, Quality Meeting, and Site Logistics Meeting. Each of these meetings will have their own list of attendees, set of agenda topics, outcomes, etc. Each will require a knowledgeable person chairing them and making sure the decisions are carried out afterwards. Because of the complexity of all this, some overall management in advance can save a lot of time and resources as the project progresses.

Project meetings: Private conversations guide

If the main thrust of the project meeting is to be brought up to date (or have the management team brought up to date), you might prefer to circulate and talk to people informally, rather than hold a more formal meeting. Or you may prefer to circulate and talk with selected people beforehand to get a sense of how they feel about the project, or what their current level of knowledge is. These conversations should take place before an update or status meeting so that any issues or discrepancies that are uncovered can be aired, discussed and hopefully resolved at the meeting itself.

Discussion items for these informal talks may include:

- Do you foresee any problems coming down the pike?
- Is there anything I should know privately about the project? These would not be discussed in the review meeting directly, but are taken on background.
- Are resources being moved away to do other jobs?
- Will that impact your job?
- Is your team working productively?
- Is your team 'happy,' and do they need anything else to work productively?
- Is there anything missing which would make your job easier?
- Is there anything else bothering you?
- Have you or your team had any ideas that might apply to other teams on this project?

A sample Project Review Meeting agenda (example: for a planned physical asset shutdown)

1. Begin with a review of safety and/or product quality issues
2. Mention any lean or sustainability items, or environmental issues which you may be trying to get people to think about for the long term
3. Scorecard: A brief review of where we are today in relation to the project schedule
4. 5 minute (or less) reports from accountability holders – updates and reviews
5. Discuss accomplishments and acknowledge good work
6. New business (problems or opportunities not presented before)
7. Detailed view of breakdowns and mitigation efforts, including requests for resources or other items needing discussion
8. Review of action items and promises made at the last Project Review Meeting

9   Quick overview of major breakdowns brewing and hot upcoming topics

10   Plans for today

11   End with safety goals and issues

Important: *Maintain an Action Promised List, perhaps on a shared resource such as a web-based file accessible to everyone. This reminds people of what they promised to do and increases the level of accountability. Meetings run more smoothly and projects move forward with less acrimony wherever a work group maintains an Action Promised List.*

Flash Meeting

This can be an ad hoc meeting called by text message or IM that convenes and then, when its work is done, everyone disperses. These instant meetings, while disruptive to the individuals, are good for quick brainstorming, straw poles (finding out where everyone is on a particular issue) or sharing breaking news.

It is based on the concept of 'Flash Mob,' first created in New York in 2003. A flash mob is a group of people who assemble suddenly in a place, perform an unusual and seemingly pointless act for a brief time, then disperse, often for the purposes of entertainment, satire, and artistic expression. The original flash mobs were organized via text, social media, or email among groups of friends or people with a common interest.

In our context a Flash Meeting should be short (10-15 minutes), focused on a limited goal and not overused (or no one will get any work done). The reasons for calling a Flash Meeting should be easy to understand and spelled out ahead of time.

Safety meetings (mandated meetings)

In the US, holding periodic safety meetings is mandated by OSHA (the Occupational Safety and Health Administration).

OSHA "requires that all companies hold regular safety meetings for both management and employees. The type of meeting that a company must hold to comply with OSHA regulations varies depending on its size and industry; however, companies must adhere to the safety meeting requirements to remain in business. A company found not in compliance with OSHA regulations may face a fine or have its operating license revoked." (www.ehow.com)

These meetings have to be scheduled and held on company time. The topics would include at least the hazards that your organization faces. The meeting could even include home hazards and driving hazards. In factories and construction sites, the safety meeting can be tagged onto the toolbox meeting. This is (usually) a quick morning meeting to discuss the work of the day. It is also designed to highlight some of the special hazards (such as crane lifts). Some of the topics for a toolbox meeting might include:

- Behavioral safety
- Confined space
- Disease prevention
- Electrical hazards
- Ergonomics
- Hearing conservation
- Ladders

- Fatigue
- Fire
- Forklifts
- General

- Hazard communications: Hazcom, MSDS sheets, labeling and the like
- Lifting toolbox: topics about lifting and general back care
- LOTO: Lockout and Tagout associated toolbox topics
- Office issues
- PPE: topics involving personal protective equipment
- Seasonal toolbox topics dealing with seasonal issues or holiday awareness
- Slips, trips and falls

- Small tools toolbox topics associated with small hand or powered tools.
- Weather and how it affects safety

Each meeting has an agenda, attendance list and is signed by the provider (facilitator or employee leading the meeting). Records must be kept and made available to an OSHA inspector on request.

SAFETY MEETING RECORD

Person Conducting _____   Department/Area _____

Date/Time _____   Number Attending _____

Attendees:

_____   _____   _____
_____   _____   _____
_____   _____   _____
_____   _____   _____
_____   _____   _____

CONTENT

What was the main topic? _____

What were the subtopics? _____

What questions or concerns were expressed? _____

_____
_____
_____
_____
_____
_____
_____

Safety item reviewed _____

_____
_____
_____

Meetings with lawyers and other expensive professionals

Sometimes the meeting is with people who are paid by the hour. These meetings can get very expensive. It is essential to keep some control over the topics and to be sure you've covered the points for which the meeting would be called.

- Treat your first meeting as a business consultation. Be professional and be aware they will be trying to impress you and you them.
- It is ok to spend some time getting to know them and they you but manage the time in view of the assignment.
- Try to supply information before the meeting so they are not coming in blind and have had some thoughts about you, your concerns and your organization.
- While a formal agenda might not be needed, a list of the meeting deliverables is required. This includes questions you have, opinions that you would like, topics covered and assignments.
- Minutes or notes are also essential. You can be sure they will make notes from the meetings but you should also.
- After you have laid out the facts, shut-up and be sure you listen – they are the experts.
- Be sure to note who is to follow through with what materials which were promised and by when.

Chapter 3

Meeting culture and ground rules

Good meetings result when someone sets a goal for the meeting, brings the right people together under the right conditions, and keeps people moving forward in a productive, cohesive way. All this does not happen by chance. It comes about by using well thought out procedures and sticking to them, even when the temptations are strong to vary or meander away.

Meeting Etiquette

Definition: *The dictionary defines meeting as coming face-to-face or coming together for a common purpose.* The face-to-face part of the definition is less important than the intention of promoting the common purpose. Today people can use technology to gather their thoughts and ideas together without being face-to-face. They can attend the meeting by phone, videoconference or over the Internet in order work together on a common cause.

What do you call people who attend the meeting? Formally they are often called attendees; however these terms imply a kind of passive role for people. Instead, consider calling them participants. It ups the game to have everyone participating. Merely being there does little to promote the common purpose.

According to the dictionary, etiquette is defined as "the rules and conventions governing correct or polite behavior in society in general or in a specific social or professional group or situation." At one time etiquette distinguished the upper crust from everyone else, who didn't have the means, the energy or the training from childhood to behave politely toward others.

Etiquette grew out of a need for people to interact in a positive way, avoiding unnecessary conflict, and managing the conflicts that did occur, all while feeling good about themselves and the people they interacted with. Business etiquette developed out of much the same need. It has evolved to be somewhat less formal, but has continued to remain a vibrant tradition while formal etiquette has to a great extent faded from everyday life.

Lyudmila Bloch, an international etiquette expert, protocol consultant, seminar leader and author, writes, "Business etiquette is a philosophy of building and fostering business relations based on trust, integrity, best practices, and cultural and regional sensitivities. Business etiquette is not a 'business behavior code' – it can be defined only as 'guiding principles for success in business.'"

This is an excellent starting point for a definition of meeting etiquette. We will take meeting etiquette to be the sum of the rules, conventions, behavior and attitudes that "foster business relations based on trust, integrity, best practices, and cultural and regional sensitivities." These ideas can provide guiding principles for success in our businesses and organizations.

Keep in mind that some of these etiquette rules might be helpful guides only for a particular type of meeting in a particular part of the world. Etiquette for the most part is showing courtesy to others, and what is courteous in one region may be considered rude elsewhere.

Gary M. Smith created some etiquette rules based on his extensive work with groups, including these meeting basics:

- *R.S.V.P.:* When asked via phone, email, or electronic calendar to attend a business meeting, reply within one business day if a reply is requested. Some meetings are structured and space may be secured on the basis of expected attendance. If invitees show up without warning, or fail to show up after promising to attend, they may cost the organization needless dollars, or require the entire meeting to scramble for a new location.

- *Arrive early.* If this is not possible, arrive at the scheduled time at the latest – but never late. Do not assume that the beginning of a meeting will be delayed until all those planning to attend are present. This penalizes the early birds, and begins a culture of ever-later meeting participants, a situation which erodes everyone's trust in their fellow workers.

- *If you must be late:* When you arrive late, you risk missing valuable information and lose the chance to provide your input. You should not expect others to fill you in during or after the meeting. Recaps during the meeting make it hard for everyone else to hear the main part of the meeting. Recaps afterward are a burden on others; everyone is busy, and those who were conscientious enough to arrive on time should not have to return to their other responsibilities even later in order to bring you up to speed.

- *Come prepared.* Always bring something to write on as well as something to write with. Meetings usually are called to convey information, and it is disruptive to ask others for paper and pen, or to borrow their laptop, if you decide you want to take notes. If you know you will be presenting information, make sure ahead of time that your handouts, PowerPoints, etc., are organized and ready.

- *Do not interrupt.* Hold your comments for the speaker until the meeting adjourns or until the speaker asks for comments, unless the speaker has encouraged open discourse throughout the meeting. Similarly, do not interrupt other attendees. Hold your comments for others in the meeting until after the meeting is adjourned, or until you are offered a turn to speak. Interruptions and side-conversations during a meeting are disruptive to other attendees and inconsiderate of the speaker.
- *Speak in turn.* When asking a question, it usually is more appropriate to raise your hand than to blurt out your question. Other attendees may have questions, and the speaker needs to acknowledge everyone.
- *Keep your questions brief, on topic and to the point.* When asking questions, be succinct and clear. If your question is detailed, break it into parts or several questions. But be sure to ask only one question at a time; others may have questions as well.
- *Be patient and calm.* Do not fidget, drum your fingers, tap your pen, flip through or read materials on topics not covered in the meeting. You may be focused only on your own impatience, but for others, this disrupts their ability to concentrate and participate.
- *Attend the entire meeting.* Leave only when the meeting is adjourned. Leaving before the end of the meeting – only if absolutely necessary and with prior permission – can be disruptive to other attendees and inconsiderate of the speaker.

You will notice Mr. Smith's list is no more than good manners and consideration, corresponding closely with the ground rules discussed later in this section. Manners went out of style for a few decades but now seem to be coming back into business conversations.

Day one (at the beginning of the first meeting in a series)

One of the most important ways to establish good meeting procedures is during the first meeting for any group. Especially if the participants are not regular meeting participants, or don't know each other well, it is essential to get off on the right foot. A key goal of the first meeting is to affirm the goals of the group and establish ground rules/communication lines for how the team should operate. It is crucial to establish the following, at minimum:

- ***A name for your team or group*** – This may sound trivial but having a common name can give a group coherence and help the members feel closer to the project. Choosing a name is a simple task that can be used to establish meeting procedures; beyond that, it gives coherence and common identity to previously diverse members of an organization. And if members come up with a "cool" name, it will help motivate them and keep a smile on their faces.
- ***Share contact information*** – You will probably want to share e-mail addresses and possibly phone numbers. You should also establish when and how different communication tools should be used.
- Establish a timeline, roles and responsibilities.
- Set ground rules (below) and review them together. This establishes expectations, and having the review helps the chairman keep the group from descending into chaos later.
- Allow people to fully introduce themselves. Sometimes we might share a meeting with someone and know next to nothing about them. Also it might be useful to share what they are working on or what's on their mind.

Setting ground rules

Although disagreements will arise, it is possible to voice opinions in such a way so that conflicts do not escalate (conflict itself can enliven meetings, but if it is not contained appropriately, it can devastate the sense of common purpose and the ability to work together.). Teams often develop ground rules that extend to how they want a meeting conducted.

Some possible team ground rules include:
- Start and end meetings on time.
- Attend all meetings. Be on time.
- Agreements such as:
    - When we are invited to a meeting, we will accept or decline the invitation. If we accept, we guarantee our presence unless there is an emergency, in which case we will have someone notify the chair before the start of the meeting.
    - Job titles and rank are left at the door (to encourage honest feedback and contribution).
    - We will use group time wisely, respecting each other by starting on time, returning from breaks and ending our meetings promptly.
    - We will keep the focus on our common goals, avoiding sidetracking, personality conflicts and hidden agendas. We will acknowledge problems and deal with them.
    - Keep to the current topic.
    - We will avoid side-bar discussions while others are talking.
    - Commitment is demonstrated when members understand and accept their responsibilities, and tasks are achieved. Absenteeism is permitted if scheduled in advance with the leader (or an emergency).
    - When members miss a meeting, we will share the respon-

sibility for bringing them up to date.

- Thank people for attending and for their participation.
- We will agree about the need for confidentiality. We may want information discussed in our group to remain confidential. With regards to peoples' opinions, what's said here stays here.

- Phones must be set on vibrate, instead of allowing them to ring or beep during meetings. All texting, tweeting, answering E-mail or taking phone calls in the room are banned unless a particular communication is crucial to the topic at hand.
- Keep records of the team's compiled work (minutes) - this will make it less likely participants will "forget" what went on in previous meetings.
- Value the diversity of team members.
- Keep everyone up-to-date on developments affecting the common work.
- If there are guests at the meeting, introduce them and their role.

Ground rules: Meeting Processes

- Have fun! Yes, you may be having a serious discussion but life is too short to get hung up on it. Ideally everyone should leave the meeting feeling better for it and that their involvement was critical to its success.
- When possible, make decisions by consensus of all necessary team members. Some meetings may have legal requirements about the votes required to make decisions.
- Members should know (regarding more informal meetings) that any team member may modify or add to an agenda (before the meeting).
- Summarize decisions and future plans before everyone leaves. The leader or another team member should sum-

marize what was decided, the current status of the project, and make sure each item in the agenda was covered. This catches many oversights that might be missed otherwise.

- Be prepared to drop a topic - If a team gets stuck on a topic, it may be wise to delay discussion of it for another time or assign it to a sub-group or person.
- When you have a problem to solve, use the 5-why technique. Ask why five times (peal the onion layer by layer).
- Communicate, communicate, communicate - before, during and after the meeting - to make sure that action items are properly documented, resolved, and assigned to a responsible individual and given a due date.
- Cancel any meetings not needed!

Ground rules: Participation

- Be supportive rather than judgmental. Focus on the task and process and not on personalities involved.
- Everybody has the right to sit and listen ("lurking") during formative stages of the team and even from time to time later during the team's operation. Do not deny people their "think time."
- Give feedback directly and openly, in a timely fashion. Provide information that is specific and focuses on the task or process.
- No one should feel silenced. If they do, they should take it up with the chair/ facilitator.
- Don't interrupt another person who is talking. One person talks at a time.
- We are each responsible for what we get from this team experience.
- Practice self-respect and mutual respect.
- Build self-esteem for yourself and for one another.

- No finger pointing -- address the process, not the individual.
- Criticize only ideas, not people. (Say, "I disagree with that conclusion," instead of, "Don't be stupid.")
- Watch for "trigger words" -- language IS important.
- If need be, agree to disagree.
- Be open to new concepts and to concepts presented in new ways. Keep an open mind. Appreciate other points of view.
- Do not accept the first idea presented – wait to hear the second, third, fourth.
- Everyone is responsible for the success of the meeting.
- Be an Adventurer (leader in forwarding the action in the meeting), not a Prisoner.
- Everyone is expected to help facilitate, critique, and evaluate the meeting.
- Everyone is expected participate, and to respect and support the right to be heard.
- Be willing to forgive.
- Share air time.
- Work from you own "leading edge" and acknowledge that others are at different places
- Expect to change your own mind, but don't expect to change another's mind.
- Ensure every member participates at least once every hour.
- Include everyone in the discussion. Share the limelight.
- Encourage everyone to participate in the meeting. This is essential since the process depends on all different kinds of contributions. A crazy contribution said in jest by one person might stimulate a thought in someone else that solves the problem.
- Handle differences or conflicts in an open and positive fashion.

- Be a team player. Respect each other's ideas. Question and participate.
- Relax. Be yourself. Be honest.
- Be willing to make mistakes or have an unpopular opinion.
- Accept personal responsibility for team outcomes.
- Share your knowledge, experience, time and talents.
- Stay focused on the task and the person of the moment.
- Work on providing 100% of your focus and attention while meeting.
- Pay attention to everyone speaking; have an open mind (and a closed mouth).
- Consider the strategy of other societies that have talking sticks (props) which are passed around the table so everyone contributes something. Or simply go around the room giving everyone a chance to speak.

Part of effective participation is listening
- Make sure you understand what is being said and why it is being said. Speak up if you think you missed a crucial point.
- Practice both active and reflective listening. Before making your point, confirm to the group that you have understood the views of others by restating their point in your own words and seeking agreement that you truly understand the prior points.
- Frequently check for understanding. Summarize and paraphrase frequently to ensure that what is being said is being heard and understood. Work towards explaining consensus.
- Ask a question whenever you have one. Others may wonder the same thing.

- Feel free to share an illustration, if only to test your understanding of the points being discussed.
- Request an example if a point is not clear.

Ground rules: Meeting wrap-up

- About 15 minutes before the scheduled conclusion of the meeting, ask yourself, are we where we want to be, or are we still on a roll?
- If you have to run overtime and everyone can't stay, you should break up the meeting. Do not send the signal that one member's contribution is more important than another's – close the meeting even if the departing member says to carry on.
- If the purpose of the meeting is to reach a decision, make sure the decision maker is actually at the meeting and that the required people who need to provide inputs are present or adequately represented.
- If the results of the meeting have an effect on others who were not present, it is considered proper business etiquette to inform them of the changes.
- Group Critique – do so openly at the conclusion of the meeting and as needed throughout, by asking:
- Are there things you liked or did not like?
- How can we do them differently next time?

This list has been adapted from the work of Phil Richardson.

Chapter 4

Agenda and subject matter

Agenda: *In the beginning there was the agenda...*

The agenda is the backbone of any meeting. A well-organized agenda sets a strong foundation for your meetings; in contrast, a poorly conceived agenda can cripple you. There are four essential parts to any agenda:

- People in attendance
- Topics to be covered
- Logistics
- Timing

The meeting's **order of topics** can be important. We want to choose topics and organize them so that the meeting has a clear beginning, middle and end. Your heavy duty or controversial topics might not sit too well in the beginning or at the end of the meeting. Many meeting planners schedule the most important items second or third on the agenda to accommodate stragglers while still covering those topics when everyone is still pretty fresh. Too early and you won't have established the camaraderie necessary for non-acrimonious discussion. Too late and the energy and focus needed for discussions are already lagging.

Setting up the meeting and any discussions of process, including changes to the agenda, updates from previous meetings, etc., should go first as a way to define the meeting and bring people's attentions from outside matters to the matters to be discussed within the group. Summations, planning for future meetings, and announcements should be reserved for the end of the meeting.

Two special situations

There are two situations where you might want to ignore or modify the agenda (or cancel the meeting). One situation is a national tragedy or big news story. In this case if the meeting cannot be delayed or rescheduled, you might allow people to share in order to get it out of their system and see if you can then proceed with the business of the meeting. The risk here is that no one will pay attention to the topics being discussed.

The second situation is when there is big news within your company, or a large customer or vendor. This would include mergers, layoffs, disasters, labor actions, legal actions, health issues or death of leaders. In this case the news might have a direct effect on you and your team. You might want to reschedule if you need some time to absorb the news. If necessary, be prepared to redo the agenda completely. The risk here is both the lack of attention and the possibility that the news will overrun the business of the meeting.

Logistics and timing

The meeting agenda could be considered an agreement among team members, thus all team members should have the opportunity to provide input in the agenda (particularly for ad hoc meetings). Obviously we cannot have the chaos of everyone shouting out their own ideas throughout every meeting, but the ability to know you can contribute and argue your case when you need to is important. People should submit requests for agenda modifications well in advance wherever possible, giving the leader time to incorporate them into his/her plan for the meeting.

The agenda:

- Can be viewed as a roadmap for the meeting, complete with stops and landmarks
- Can be used as a checklist to make sure every topic is covered
- Is a reminder system for promises made at the last meeting
- Can serve as a reminder for people who are scheduled to present (make sure they prepare their presentation)
- Give people a heads-up about the topics for discussion so they can do their own research
- Lets participants know when the meeting is over

If you are the chairperson designing the agenda, keep the desired outcomes in mind. You know what you are trying to accomplish. You have decided a meeting is the best way to accomplish this. You've asked yourself what topics are important to cover and thought through the time needed to accomplish your objectives. Now, set up the roadmap to accomplish what needs to be done.

Structure

The meeting agenda should include:
- Date, time and location of meeting. Sending additional reminders the day before the meeting or even the morning of, may be wise in some cases.
- Who to contact and how to contact them about this meeting (if you will be late, for example). Be sure to have a mechanism to accept or decline the invitation to the meeting.

- List of participants expected (including guests with contact information and role). It may be all team members by default, but sometimes only a few need to be there to discuss a specific issue. The best way to get the right people to attend is to make sure they know about the meeting in enough time to arrange their schedules. Be rigorous about this practice; ensuring the right people show up can make or break the meeting.
- Be ruthless about who you invite (so you don't waste anyone's time). Who is in the room is as important as what is discussed.
- Purpose of the meeting (information sharing, problem solving, decision making, coordination, planning, etc.)
- Order of business to be conducted at the meeting (the agenda!) for each topic:
- Title or topic
- Short description of the topic
- Person responsible for the item (lead)
- Time allotted
- List of reference documents specifically related to the item (if applicable)
- Invitation to submit items to the chair for inclusion to agenda (if appropriate for the type of meeting). Include deadlines for submissions.

Topics can include:
- Standing items such as current status of budget, approval of old minutes, etc.
- Old business for topics brought forward from previous meetings
- New business (should have been communicated to the meeting chair before the meeting)

- Wrap-up items such as next meeting time, announcements, summary, summary of actions requested/promised
- Where to find general background or support materials required
- Minutes of the previous meeting and any specific pre-meeting assignments.

For many meetings you may want to make sure you leave additional time for open discussion. This allows the team to discuss any ongoing issues that the leader may not be aware of.

On the other hand, it is better to schedule 50 minutes of work into a 1 hour slot and let people out early than it is to schedule 50 minutes of work into a 45 minute slot and keep people late. Overall, in designing the agenda it is wise to consider the effect of agenda items on the group in four dimensions: difficulty of the subject matter, time required, energy and emotional engagement.

Now this may seem like a lot of work to prepare all this and get it to everyone in advance. It is a lot of work. But it is a good practice for a number of reasons. First, the time the meeting organizers spend in advance will keep the meeting short and more productive for all those attending the meeting. Thus what is a lot of work for one person saves time for many (remember the leverage effect).

In the project planning world, an hour spent in effective planning typically results in 3-5 fewer hours of execution time. The same seems to hold true for meeting planning.

Second, the discipline of thinking out the agenda in advance will help winnow out those topics which do not need everyone involved, again to avoid wasting many people's time. Third, having thought through the items and warned people ahead of time, the objectives will be clear and the meeting more focused, with fewer people complaining they weren't prepared to discuss the topics on the agenda.

In practice, some of the steps above will be skipped for many of your meetings. But the more you follow those procedures, the more you will come to appreciate their importance. And the more you follow them, the faster and more automatic they will become. Good meeting practice pays big dividends!

Circadian rhythms

Circadian rhythms are physical, mental and behavioral changes that follow a roughly 24-hour cycle, responding primarily to light and darkness in an organism's environment. They are found in most living things, including animals, plants and many tiny microbes. The study of circadian rhythms is called chronobiology. http://www.nigms.nih.gov/Education/Factsheet_CircadianRhyt hms.htm) (National Institutes of Health)

People have evolved over millions of years to have cyclical energy patterns throughout the day. Your meeting schedule should, when possible, support rather than fight these circadian rhythms. Most people who work during business hours or on a day shift have stronger energy in the mornings and late afternoons, with a sag in energy levels in the early afternoon.

Accordingly, you should assume that an after-lunch meeting will be a snoozefest unless it is full of active, fun, enlivening topics. On the other hand, if you want to manage the length of a meeting, keeping it short and succinct, schedule it 20 minutes before lunch or before people go home for the day.

A well designed, fast paced, short morning meeting will leave the people energized and wanting to face the day. If the same meeting is slow and long with sweets and coffee the people will need a few hours to recover!

Simplified template for constructive meetings

Meeting Title			
Logistics			
Time:			
Date:			
Participants:			
Please Bring/Read:			
Remote Telephone details:			
Purpose			
New Business			

Item	Time	Agenda Item	Presenter
1			
2			
3			
4			

Old Business and Open Actions

No	Action/Discussion	Who	When	Status or comment
1.				
2.				
3.				
4.				

Next Meeting Details:

Meeting Agenda

Meeting Subject:

Meeting Organizer: Start Date: Start Time:
                            7/30/2003

Location: End Date: End Time:
                            7/30/2003

Objective

Agenda Items

                                          Owner: Time Allotted:

1   [Type a subject for this agenda item.]

    [Type a description or details for this agenda item.]

Action Items

Action Title	Action Owner	Priority	Progress	Due Date
		None	Not Started	

○ Click here to insert the Materials Provided section

○ Click here to insert the Materials to Bring section

Attendee Information

Name	E-mail Address	Required
		☑

[Send Meeting Agenda]

Sample Template from Microsoft Office Templates:

Idea for action: *Store the minutes, action lists and other meeting resources on a shared drive or cloud-based file system (such as dropbox.com). Display the URL or path on the meeting notices so everyone can access them.*

Remember: Agendas only work when they are followed! *All the more reason to have some discussion of the agenda itself at the top of the agenda for your meetings.*

Chapter 5

Notes and Minutes

Functions

Minutes, or meeting notes, are an instant (taken at the event itself) written record of a meeting. They have two major functions in business. First, they remind people of what they agreed to do. Second, they inform the audience of what was decided by the group. (To clarify: notes and minutes are essentially the same thing. Minutes are more formal, however, and are often required by organizational bylaws.)

These records also serve several secondary functions, typically:
- To provide a list of attendees
- To describe the topics and issues discussed at the meeting
- To list comments or discussions on those issues
- Perhaps most important, to announce decisions made regarding those issues

There are big differences between minutes for a business meeting and minutes for a public hearing or board meeting. The recording of minutes for public meetings and governmental hearings follow prescribed rules and legal precedents. Improper recording of minutes can result in lawsuits, courts overturning decisions made by government officials, even sanctions taken against meeting attendees. Thus most public agencies have minutes taken by personnel specially trained in the legal requirements. Board meetings generally have legal requirements defined in the organization's bylaws which have legal effects beyond just the issues covered at the meeting. If improperly recorded, these may result in lawsuits through the civil courts.

In public venues, speakers' words may be recorded verbatim (somewhat like court reporting), so that every speaker's comments are included. In the U.S. Congress, speakers sometimes submit speeches that weren't even spoken for recording into the public record.

No minutes = wasted meeting?

Beyond any legal requirements for minutes, minutes are important for keeping a common record of what occurred during the meeting. If the minutes don't accurately reflect what happened, if they weren't taken at all, or if they were taken but are undecipherable, the time spent having meetings might very well be wasted. Without good meeting notes, people may not remember, recognize or agree upon:

- Decisions made in the meeting
- Who was there and who was not
- The next steps to be taken
- Action items

And when people can't remember or agree upon the items above, they end up going in different directions. The result is chaos, wasted time and resources, and probably having to meet again   for   the   same   original   purpose!

Memory effect

Not remembering the content of a meeting is a problem quite a bit bigger than people realize. Most people think they have a good memory and so are pretty confident they remember what happened in a meeting. They might take minimal notes and rely on their memories to fill in the blanks.

Yet how many times have you been at a meeting where a participant remembers when they walk in the door that they forgot to do something they promised at the last meeting? It is frustrating and compromises the forward motion of the group. It literally stops the action in its tracks.

And how often have you been at a meeting and when you report back to others, they say, "That's not what we agreed on." They have their version, you have your version, and everyone has to weigh in on their slightly variant memories of what happened.

Significant research has been conducted on how people remember meetings. In one study, two British psychologists recorded a discussion at a meeting of psychologists. Two weeks later they contacted all the participants and asked them to write down everything they remembered from the meeting. The accounts were checked against the recordings. Their findings:

- On average, respondents missed 90% of the specific topics covered.
- Of the ones they recalled, nearly half were substantially incorrect.
- Many participants remembered comments that were never made.
- People often converted implicit meanings to explicit meanings, or vice versa, thus subtly misremembering the assumptions, tone, etc.

The implications are clear. Be sure someone takes notes at all meetings. If the stakes are high enough, notes should be reviewed by a second person immediately to make sure they are accurate.

You cannot depend on memory alone. If an important incident happens, direct everyone to immediately make notes on paper or computer to refer to later.

Dos and don'ts for writing up the minutes

Lynn Gaertner-Johnston, founder of Syntax Training in Seattle, gave some great pointers for writing up minutes in her blog:

- Write up the minutes from your notes soon after the meeting – preferably within 48 hours.
- Don't describe all the "he said, she said" details unless those details are important. Record topics discussed, decisions made, and action items.
- Don't include information that will embarrass anyone (for example, "Then Terry left the room in tears").
- Do use positive language. Rather than describing the discussion as heated or angry, use passionate, lively, or energetic – all of which are just as true as the negative words.

Some additional tips from Meetingwizard.org include ideas to speed up and simplify the notes taking process:

- Start the process ahead of time by preparing an outline based on the agenda. Leave plenty of white space for notes.
- Prepare a list of expected attendees. Check off their names as people enter the room. Alternatively you can pass around an attendance sheet for everyone to sign as the meeting starts; make sure someone passes the sheet to latecomers for them to add their names.

- Whenever new people attend, make sure to ask for introductions. This helps establish positive meeting dynamics, and helps the minutes-taker be clear about who said what.
- It may help to make a map of the seating arrangements during the meeting or when writing up the minutes, as an aid to remember who made or seconded various motions.

Ideas to tighten up the minute-taking process

- Consider having minutes approved by the chair or facilitator before distributing them to the attendees.
- For formal and corporate meetings, include items such as the approval of previous minutes, time of adjournment and all resolutions (this is legally important to protect people who made decisions before the meeting that have to be ratified by a board).
- Use whatever devices are comfortable for you, including a notepad, a laptop computer, a tape recorder, a steno pad or shorthand. Many people routinely record important meetings as a backup for their notes.
- Be prepared! Study the issues to be discussed and ask any clarifying questions ahead of time. If you have to fumble for understanding while you are taking notes, they won't make any sense to you later.

Newbie note takers

For people new to the role of minute taker, it is essential to understand the bigger picture, especially what kind of information is essential to report and make part of the record. We suggest you read minutes from prior meetings. In fact, if you can find minutes for this meeting going back several months or even years, it might be useful to read randomly selected minutes, even from the distant past. This research will pay off in your understanding of the procedures and issues faced currently, and how they should be recorded.

Answer these questions in your minutes

To avoid wasting time, be sure your notes and minutes answer these 9 questions:

1 Location, date and time of meeting?
2 For all meetings: Who attended? Some meetings: Who was absent? Few meetings: Who communicated absence beforehand?
3 Agenda going in?
4 What topics ended up being discussed?
5 What decisions were made? Some meetings: Minority opinions and discussion that lead to decision.
6 Actions items. Who is to complete the action, and by what date?
7 Copies or a link available to any material handed out (reports, budgets, etc.)?
8 Is there anything special the reader of the minutes should know or do?
9 Next meeting: When? Where? What topics to be covered? Why?

Technology to the rescue: One useful tool is called the Livescribe smart pen and recording system. This system uses a smart pen and special paper. Anything that is written on the special pad can be saved as a file. The pen also records the entire meeting as a MP3 file (transferable to your computer). One great benefit of such technology is the ability to verify youotes by listening to the actual meeting. If you are unclear of your notes, you can tap any section of the notes with the special pen and replay that part of the meeting. The whole package is under $200.

Examples of templates

A simplified Minutes format

This format is excellent for action oriented meetings. Its advantage is that in very few words you can describe the actions to be taken. And in a very few seconds the attendees can view what they are supposed to do to forward the actions of the group and when they are expected to be finished.

Name of Organization: Purpose of Meeting: Date/Time: Chair:				
Topic	Discussion	Action	Person Responsible	By when
1. Preprint agenda topics here. Leave a lot of space	Just major points. Not details	This item should be written in clear action language so there is no doubt what was volunteered, decided or assigned. If it was a discussion without an action item, leave blank	Important to have someone "accountable" for each action item. If it just a discussion, leave blank	Next meeting? Date?
2. As above				

This format can be made part of a larger meeting minutes structure. Some additional items could include participants, discussions and minority opinions, abstentions in votes on important issues, reports, and items that were tabled for a subsequent meeting.

A more complete minutes format

The template below was modified from Office.microsoft.com. The Office site has a wealth of templates for all kinds of business purposes including those shown below:

Meeting Title		
Minutes	[Meeting Date] [Meeting Time]	[Meeting Location]
MEETING CALLED BY		
TYPE OF MEETING		
FACILITATOR		
NOTE TAKER		
TIMEKEEPER		
ATTENDEES		
Agenda topics (This section would be duplicated as needed)		
[Time allotted]	[Agenda topic]	[Presenter]
DISCUSSION		
CONCLUSIONS		
ACTION ITEMS	PERSON RESPONSIBLE	DEADLINE
OBSERVERS		
RESOURCE PERSONS		
SPECIAL NOTES		

None of this relieves you of the responsibility to also take your own notes!

Action Management

In some cases no formal minutes are required, just a list of actions decided on. When actions are decided by the group, they can be recorded into an action management system. This can be a simple table (such as the following) or a piece of an elaborate project management system.

Name of Organization or Group: Purpose of Meeting: Date/Time: Chair:		
ACTION MANAGEMENT		
Action	Person Responsible	By when
This item should be written in clear action language so there is no doubt what was volunteered, decided or assigned.	It is important to have someone who is account-able for each action item.	Next meeting? Date?
Next action - ordered by date or priority		
Next...		

Tabled items might be added to a list of all items tabled (and removed when the topic is reintroduced from the table or removed from consideration). New items are inserted at the top of the table

Name of Organization:	
Purpose of Meeting:	
Date/Time:	
Chair:	
Tabled Topics Listing	
Topic	When Tabled
What was the motion (formal meetings) or topic to be delayed to some future time? New topics are inserted here.	Date tabled
Next older tabled item (date ordered – oldest on bottom) .	Date tabled
Next... Periodically clean this list and remove obsolete items.	Date tabled

Chapter 6

Roles people play (in meetings)

We have briefly discussed roles and responsibilities at meetings. In this chapter we will flesh out some of these roles: participant, timekeeper, note taker, chair or facilitator.

Some general ideas for consideration about roles and responsibilities at meetings:

- Consider periodic rotation of responsibilities. This allows each member to learn to respect each other's roles, improving cooperation during meetings.
- Allow the note taker to participate in the conversation, but make sure that the material being discussed is still captured.
- Note taker: take notes which are clear, concise, complete, and accurate. Do not place the entire burden for documenting the meeting on a recording device.
- Publish the agenda beforehand and outcomes afterwards. This makes it more likely that people come prepared for the topics to be covered, and improves agreement and accountability for tasks moving forward.

- Provide key points to participants.
- Review and agree on the agenda at the start of meeting and then stick to it. But ...
- Do not be fanatical about it; e.g., go with the flow – if things are progressing and relevant ideas are flowing, keep it rolling.

The masterful meeting participant

A good participant participates in and contributes in a positive fashion to the meeting. In fact, without **good participants, there is no way to have an effective meeting.** Being a master meeting participant takes training in being able to contribute in a variety of circumstances. Particularly:

- Be prepared for the meeting. Make sure you have read all materials, viewed all messages, visited all the links and bring hard copies or electronic versions of documents with you (in a folder, notebook or iPad-type device).
- Come to the meeting on time. If you know you will be late and can send off an e-mail or text message before the meeting starts, you should do so. Don't worry about bothering the chair; it is common courtesy to let him or her know who will be there at any meeting they are in charge of.
- Participate enthusiastically in the meeting. Even if you're not a talker, other team members may need reassurance that you are following the discussion and are listening.
- Do not interrupt when someone else is talking.
- Don't shoot down other people's ideas. Be willing to consider them on their merits. Even if you disagree, there may be some crumb of usefulness in even the most unexpected suggestions.

- Be respectful and open. No "kill" statements ("That is the dumbest thing I ever heard of!")
- Value the diversity of team members. Unless the member is a "shirker," (e.g. never attends meetings or does their share of work), then each person has something to contribute to the team. Make sure you know what it is.

There are four positive personalities or roles that meeting participants can adopt. Each one has a job to do when needed for success of the meeting. These categories are described by Hanscom and Pugaczewki in their slides on board meetings:

- The Initiator is a person who can get the ball rolling, break the ice and speak first
- The Reconciler helps treat wounds to egos and diffuses conflict
- The Scout keeps the group on the path and returns it when it goes astray
- The Optimist always sees the positive side of issues

Note: *That any participant may switch roles during a meeting, fulfilling different functions at different times. Yet many, by nature, tend to play only one or two of these roles, depending on their own propensities and personalities.*

These positive roles go far in creating a dynamic, well-functioning meeting. Thus it is useful for the group as a whole when people study, even train or practice taking on one of these positive roles. However there are other roles, which we might call negative roles, which people can slip into, especially when meetings get contentious. These negative roles tend to create dissonance and bad feelings within a group, thus interfering with the productivity of meetings.

Most of the time we want to manage or avoid the personality types that interfere with the forward motion of the meeting. Look out for:

- The Aggressor who challenges everything. When confronted with such a personality or behavior, try to channel the aggression into a useful direction – toward marshaling energies to attack waste, rework, energy usage, etc.
- The Interrupter, who can't wait to insert their opinion (even if it duplicates what others have said).
- The Hijacker, who wants the plane but wants to go somewhere else (brings their own agenda).

Look out for these negative patterns, even if the person following them is you! Note that there is a place for these people at the table, especially if their energy and focus can be redirected or reoriented to a position or cause which will help forward the purposes of the group.

There are additional behaviors or personalities that participants may display which are neither positive or negative, but neutral. These will neither forward the action nor clog it up, but too many of them at one meeting can nonetheless bog things down. Sometimes the facilitator will need to get in the neutral participants' faces to encourage them to push the cart (meeting) out of the mud:

- The Clam is quiet. Sometimes they may be having deep and relevant thoughts; sometimes they may be thinking about motor oil, or the pleasures of the previous night.
- The Talker is disruptive because they start or maintain side conversations.
- The Joker is a jester who distracts the group, sometimes for good, often for ill.
- The Expert may know something relevant to the topic

under discussion, but may need to be reined in when they go on too long, too deeply, or about too many distracting secondary considerations.

The masterful meeting participant takes positive roles most of the time. If they find themselves sliding into neutral or negative roles, they quickly reverse themselves and return to making a positive contribution to the meeting. If someone else calls them on taking a negative role, they graciously acknowledge the temporary slippage and return to positivity.

Minder/Timekeeper

If the agenda has times written next to the topics, the minder/timekeeper reminds the meeting facilitator to keep the flow moving forward. Some minders face the chair (sitting across the table) and have signs already made up with "10 minutes" or "5 minutes to go" or "Call for overtime," etc. They can be assigned to help manage individual topics or the entire meeting.

The minder may use subtle signals directed towards the chairperson, such as a gesture, or can actively help manage the meeting. The minder might also make phone calls or send texts at the request of the chair as necessary to support the meeting.

Scribe/note taker

Most meetings need notes or formal minutes of topics, decisions, requests and promises. Since the intersection between the meeting and reality is the action list, managing that is of paramount importance. See the preceding discussion on minutes.

In specialized meetings such as project or problem solving meetings, or meetings using brainstorming techniques, there might be a note taker and a different person called a scribe. They would be located near the facilitator by a white board or flip chart. The scribe makes comments, pictures, and diagrams (such as the cause tree in a Root Cause Analysis meeting). Their role is to capture, preserve and continuously display ideas and important comments. They should have some training in methods of mental mapping and brainstorming. In some cases the facilitator acts as the scribe.

Note: *A simple sketch on paper or a dry erase board immediately provides the group with a picture that everyone can edit, improve, point at and comment on. Don't overlook the importance of a simple sketch.*

The Chair and the Facilitator

Three factors determine the quality and effectiveness of your meetings. We've discussed the participants and the organizational culture elsewhere. The single biggest determinant of the meeting quality and tenor is the chair or facilitator. A skilled facilitator or chair can overcome most dysfunctions in the other factors.

The chair owns the meeting. They pick the time, venue and (may) dictate the agenda. Usually the Chair holds the highest status in the room, while a facilitator is a professional trained to get the most out of all the people in the room. In some cases the Chair and the Facilitator are the same person (especially within traditional organizations). In the section below you can see that there is a significant amount of overlap in their respective functions. The chair or facilitator has to manage the variety of personalities and roles attending the meeting. In some cases they might have to rearrange seats or have a private talk with certain people to enable the rest of the group to focus on the agenda items.

Chair

The chairman, chairperson or "Chair" is the person who physically runs the meeting. The Chair has several privileges or responsibilities. In addition to keeping the meeting running smoothly and making sure the objectives of the meeting are met, he or she usually decides in advance the time, place and agenda for the meeting. These details would be distributed by the Chair or his/her representative.

The Chair enforces the ground rules, without which the meeting can easily fall into chaos or acrimony. Many of the ground rules (discussed previously) are simply good etiquette to ensure that people treat each other with respect.

Some helpful ideas for the Chair:
- Meetings tend to run more smoothly and get more accomplished when people know:
  - Why they are meeting
  - How much time they need to set aside to meet
  - What they need to pull together in advance for the sake of achieving the common purposes of the group
- The Chair does a better job in the long run if they role-model the ground rules by being organized, listening intently, not taking calls or texts and being sure to relay the proper information so people are not taken by surprise (it is bad business etiquette to publicly embarrass your coworkers if it can be avoided).
- A meeting may run more efficiently if the Chair considers in advance any potential landmines and comes up with potential solutions.
  - Known rivalries may be provoked when comparison statistics are provided. Consider how these rivalries may be redirected along paths which are productive instead of destructive for the group as a whole.

- Unexpected tasks may need assignment or volunteers to take them on. Consider the strengths of your team members and who might actually enjoy or benefit from picking up this additional workload.
- Unexpected cutbacks may need to be allocated. Consider:
  - Soliciting solutions from among your team members, who may have come up with efficiency ideas you haven't considered.
  - Inviting the group to consider the overall picture, and stressing that the cutbacks should be allocated fairly or with the least harm to the mission of the organization.

The chair should also have a sense of any hidden agendas. Many times (throughout history) the chair, head, king or prime minister was the last person to figure out the hidden agendas of the participants. A good chair should ask questions and communicate with people outside the meeting and either be plugged into the grapevine or have a trusted contact who is plugged in.

We know almost everyone has a private or personal agenda. It might be to look good, to advance, to impress this person or that, or even get revenge for real or imagined slights. The hidden agenda is only a problem if it works against the smooth operation of the meeting. Private agendas are normal and could be assumed; watch out for anyone whose private motives start to damage the meeting's integrity or harms other participants.

Remember, a key role of the chair is to ensure the meeting stays within a set framework or agenda so that the time spent away from tasks is as short and effective as possible. For further tips and tricks, see chapters 8 and 10 on facilitation.

Facilitator

We have already discussed the meeting Chair. The facilitator is the person working to get groups going in the right direction for the job at hand. The facilitator might be an outsider; often they have been professionally trained in group dynamics. But often facilitation is done by the Chair, who facilitates based on their own observations and experience, with little formal training in facilitation.

So what does a good facilitator do? We have an extensive discussion along with a list of tips and tricks for running good meetings, in the next several chapters. Ultimately, the process of facilitation is the process of running the meeting smoothly and productively, whether it is done formally by the meeting chairperson or by another person delegated to manage the meeting.

Presentations

PowerPoint as a program has a lot in common with meetings. Everybody complains about it, yet everyone uses it. Even virtual meetings are frequently run by the slide deck. Making you an expert in PowerPoint is well beyond the scope of this work, but helping you avoid the more common blunders will help the quality of your meetings. For a deeper introduction, there are many Internet based training classes (both free and paid) and other resources to improve your presentations and PowerPoint. Meanwhile, key points include:

- Know your audience, along with their their level of expertise, expectations and probable attention span.
- Know the time of day and condition of the audience (after lunch, after work)
- Pace your talk. Overheads which are dense with information should be reviewed more slowly.

- Six rule: maximum of 6 lines per slide and 6 words per line.
- Use title overheads for every major point in the presentation.
- Try special graphics and color, but keep them consistent and appropriate for the occasion.
- Use the 3T approach. Tell the participants what you are going to tell them, tell them, then tell them what you told them.
- Practice, Practice, Practice – know your material and don't read the slide or your notes. Know the order of the slides so you don't have to look at the screen to see what's next.
- Try to anticipate questions and do your homework (live practice is great).
- Define technical words and jargon on the first usage. Use language in your talk which is consistent with the overheads.
- Keep charts, text, lists simple. KISS (keep it simple stupid)
- Make one point per slide.
- Check out your room, sit in several seats, and establish light levels. Can you see the slides and read the text from anywhere in the room?
- Always face your audience while speaking. Never speak into the screen.
- Make a second copy of any slide that you have to refer to again so you can insert it into the presentation in the correct sequence.
- If you have written handouts, make sure the slides are duplicated exactly.
- Prepare yourself for something to go wrong (like keeping your presentation on a memory stick or a spare laptop).

On handouts

If you hand them out when the participants sit down, they will read the handouts rather than participate in the meeting. It might be desirable that they review the graphs or results right then. If so give time in the agenda to read and review (and possibly discuss) the materials. Otherwise, consider giving handouts to take with them at the end of the meeting.

Longer reports or documents present a problem. If they cannot be distributed ahead of time, you will have to give people time to look them over, then review what needs to be reviewed together as specifically as possible.

All handouts need page numbers, exhibit numbers, tabs and other features to make them quick to navigate and easy to use.

If you can't provide these things, it may be better not to give handouts.

Chapter 7

The use of checklists

Checklists, those mundane listings of critical tasks to be completed, are widely used in settings where the outcome is critical (e.g. aviation, power plants, medicine, military operations). Checklists have been credited with saving the lives of millions of people from settings as diverse as commercial air flights to operating rooms, as well as time and energy in many projects that otherwise might be wasted. What we might not know is that checklists can also play a prominent role in situations ranging from factories to day care centers and political campaigns.

A checklist is simply a reminder system for any complex but important undertaking. It consists of all the things that you know need coverage, and ensures they will not be forgotten or overlooked. The checklist can be used to list the practices that make a successful meeting right there in front of you until they are taken care of. That way, even if you are tired, have a headache or are preoccupied, even if you're sure you'll remember to do x, y and z, you won't miss anything important.

Checklists can also help streamline your meetings and make them run more effectively. They can help make sure the meeting is well-organized and covers all the topics which need to be covered, keeping people on track and accountable for the actions others depend on them to complete. People will leave the well-organized meeting feeling satisfied that everyone knows what they need to do, even looking forward to the next one.

You may be wondering how a checklist differs from an agenda. The checklist can cover the entire process of meeting organization, from the decision that a meeting is necessary to the follow-ups after a meeting to make sure meeting decisions are implemented. Included on the checklist will be items such as devising the agenda, making sure the meeting site is available and contains the resources required to run the meeting (enough chairs, screen projector, etc.). The agenda organizes the topics for discussion during the meeting, but the checklist organizes the organization itself so that the meeting will occur with the appropriate participants, resources, and preparation for the discussions and decisions that need to be made.

If you design a meeting checklist and then distribute it, post it at the meeting site, and follow it throughout the meeting itself, the checklist itself will do much of the work for keeping things running smoothly. Here are a few tried and true simple rules for best results:

1   The important thing is to cover the checklist in the order specified.
2   Stick to the item you are on until it is complete and you can check it off.
3   Complete the entire list before deciding if you are done.

The only exception to numbers 2 and 3 above is when the group decides that one or more items on the checklist need to be covered at a later date. This may be the result of needing additional information in order to complete them, needing additional resources or agreements, or needing more time to do them justice than the time allotted for the current meeting.

Please note that the best checklists for a meeting are simple. Remember that:

- ✓ The best checklists are contained on a single side of one piece of paper. Use a large font that is easy to read.
- ✓ The most effective checklists are short and quickly completed.
- ✓ Many can be read through in under a minute.
- ✓ Checklists typically have 7-10 items on them. More than that? You may want to reorganize your meeting check list into two or more smaller checklists with fewer items, for greater focus.
- ✓ Post the checklist in advance of the meeting
- ✓ **Use it!**

You may find that you can use the same checklist over and over again as you continue to organize and prepare for further meetings. The same checklist will help you develop a thoroughly prepared series of meetings with a consistency and reliability that you and others will be able to count on.

Yet you can also use your checklist to remind yourself to try new ideas, techniques or practices, and have your meetings evolve and change as your organizational needs evolve. You can rotate new topics or procedures into the list that you want to try out. See the sample checklist below to get started. The items in italics are suggestions which help some organizations run successful meetings.

The power of the checklist is in the execution.
It only has positive effect if we use it!

Some meeting organizers make use of additional checklists to organize other meeting-related activities. These organizational aids can track the work done in the days before the meeting, the hours immediately before the meeting, and follow-up work after the meeting is over.

Using aviation as an example, the number of tasks is so large that each step in flying a plane (preflight, landing, etc.) has a different checklist. Similarly, when organizing major military operations. But for organizing your first meeting, you may want to keep the checklist as simple as possible.

In any recurring situation, your checklists will evolve over time. Checklists get smarter and more useful by incorporating new issues that arise or practices that you've tried and want to keep using, while removing old issues that no longer arise or practices that don't work out for your group.

You can start with the basic single page checklist below and adapt it to your type and style of meetings. For ease of use, these could be made into 4 different sub-checklists.

Ideas for action:
- ✓ Modify the checklist to suit your meetings and start using it at the next meeting.
- ✓ Add items that you want to try out.

On the following page is a sample checklist. A more extensive checklist can be found in the appendix. *Italic items on the checklist are ideas that you want to remind yourself to try out.*

Meeting Checklist		Title of meeting:	
Purpose of meeting:			
Date:	Facility:	Ad hoc?	Scheduled
Done	When	Idea to improve meeting	
	Few days before meeting	Have agenda sent out well before meeting with meeting day, time, location objective and topics, arrange catering if any	
	Few days before meeting *and* maybe the day before the meeting	Remind people who have promised to complete some work for the meeting. The reminder should be at the top of the communication (like the email) and made bold so it is very hard to miss.	
	10-20 minutes before meeting	Check that: • Room is actually available. • Check to see if the room is clean, • Easel has paper (if needed), white board is there, with markers, • Any other aids (like pens and pads), catering • Check out the AV before the meeting. Verify connections (Laptop to LCD projectors and thumb drives) are useable on the computer in the conference room. • You have the latest presentations, graphs, charts • Printed materials are complete and enough are printed	
	Just before the meeting starts	Assign (or request) someone to take minutes (who is good at it).	
	Beginning of the meeting	Have people introduce themselves and their role if people don't already know everyone. *People come in the door with a variety of concerns and preoccupations. Start the meeting by asking if anyone has any concerns or worries that will interfere with concentrating on the business at hand.*	
	Throughout the meeting	When you assign tasks and responsibilities, be sure to include in the minutes who is to carry out what and by when (Who-What-By when).	
	At the end of the meeting	The chair should wrap up the meeting with a summary of any agreements or assignments of tasks, plus any agreement for futhure meetings, etc.	
		At the end of the meeting ask people if the meeting achieved the objectives and to write down any ideas for improvement.	

Chapter 8

Facilitation: Running a productive meeting

Between the pre-meeting organization, the establishment and maintenance of effective ground rules, and the checklists, we've given you many good practices to keep in mind. But that's not all; there are many considerations to balance during the course of the meeting as well. You need to be prepared to participate in, or manage a real group of people with independent lives and concerns facing real business problems.

Start off the meeting on the right foot!

As we have discussed previously, it is crucial to start your meetings on time. Failing to do this establishes the sure knowledge that the meeting leaders do not respect the time of those who have gone out of their way to show up promptly. But what happens if something unexpected comes up for meeting participants, or even for a group leader?

Say you are running late and you simply cannot make it to your own meeting. This should not be a problem for the Meeting Chair who is well organized in advance. Set up a plan ahead of time for an understudy to take over if necessary, so the meeting can still start on time. That person can make sure the room is ready, greet people, summarize the goals, have the previous meeting's minutes read and approved, etc., helping the attendees get focused and ready for when the Chair arrives. This may still come off as a bit disrespectful of the other attendees' time, but it is much better than having everyone fuming and grumbling until you show up. Kenneth Blanchard, author of the popular book, "The One Minute Manager," points out, "As a manager the important thing is not what happens when you are there, but what happens when you are not there."

Idea for action: *Pick an understudy known to the group to run the meetings in your absence (preferable someone who has been attending that meeting).*

Whether the Chair or an understudy opens the meeting, in the first few minutes several things need to be accomplished. The order is not crucial, and you may use your judgment as to what works best for your group. But make sure these things happen up front:

- If everyone does not know everyone else, have people introduce themselves, along with their role in the organization (job title) and at the meeting itself (note taker or whatever). People are usually uneasy if they don't know who they are speaking with, so it is good to diminish this discomfort and begin to establish bonds as a working group.
- In any meeting where there are guests, introduce them at the outset (to make them feel more comfortable) and have them (or you) briefly outline their role (to put the rest of the people at ease) for this meeting.
- In some circumstances it is useful to include some form of check-in with everyone answering a question such as,

"What I hope to accomplish at this meeting is", "What I am most worried about, related to this project, is," or, "the biggest thing on my mind right now (that I'll leave at the door) is ..."

> • People who rush into a meeting might be thinking about some problem or conversation they just had. The primary goal of these statements is to break people free from what they were doing so they can attend to the rest of the meeting discussions.
> • These statements may also help people focus their attention on the purpose of the meeting, demon strate the range of purposes for the meeting, or demontrate the commonality of purposes for the meeting.

- Review previous meeting minutes if relevant.
- Briefly mention the Chair's goal of the meeting, and how long it is scheduled to take. This creates a limit to the intrusion on people's times, and alleviates participants' fears that the meeting will drag on forever.
- If your customs allow people to discuss the agenda itself and add items to it, this is a good time to do that.
- Update people on any progress made towards common goals.

> •These preliminaries serve to review and update while pulling people's attention onto the topics at hand and focusing them for the topics to be dis cussed during the bulk of the meeting.

Ideas for action: *At the next meeting, start with a check-in like the one described above.*

In these first few minutes, the chair or facilitator has the opportunity to set the stage for the type, duration and tone of the meeting. Taking charge in those first few minutes greatly increases the chances of having an effective meeting; failing to take charge means it is much more difficult to achieve what you were hoping to achieve by bringing the group together.

Just another reason that the chair or facilitator should be well-organized and ready, not late or unprepared for any meetings they have called.

What to do with big news

This was discussed in Chapter 4 but we will again mention how to handle a big news event, tragedy, layoff, company sale or other event that happens right before the meeting. This is tough because everyone will be thinking about that and not the business of the meeting. In many cases the best thing to do is cancel the meeting.

The second alternative is to add the item to the agenda as appropriate and give the "official" news from the chair. People may need to process the news. A freeform discussion might follow or the chair might invite people to take turns speaking about it. Some meeting leaders ask everyone to make a brief comment, getting their thoughts out of the way so that some semblance of a return to business might be possible afterwards.

It is the leader's responsibility to gauge the emotional atmosphere of the room and see what the group needs most at that moment. This is called leadership!

The Chair may need to give the news a time limit, allowing some time for processing but making sure the business of the meeting still takes place afterwards. Make sure to note that the length of time the meeting can be expected to take will be adjusted accordingly.

The heart of the meeting

As the meeting begins, provide a brief context with an overview of agenda items and introduce the overall objective of the meeting, if you haven't already done so.

Example: "Thank you all for coming. Last week we decided to cut 15% out of the Spare Parts budget, and three of you said you would interview your people to outline which particular areas these cuts might come from. Today we are planning to go over these proposed items, discuss whether any of these cuts will result in dangerous risks in other areas, and come up with a final plan."

This provides direction for the meeting and reinforces what needs to be accomplished during this time.

A key step for facilitating good meetings is to model the behavior you want from the group. After all, each group becomes a mini-culture unto itself, and members unconsciously pick up cues on what behavior is appropriate from – who else? – the people heading the group.

If you want people to come on time, start your meetings on time. Even if all the participants haven't arrived, begin when you said you would. Adhering to the schedule sends the message that you're serious about the meeting and expect participants to arrive on time. It may be too late to affect attendance at the current meeting, but will signal people to show up promptly for the future.

If you want people to participate, make sure they know that their contributions are appreciated. There is always a risk to speaking up; make participants feel the risk was worth it, even when not everyone agrees with what they have suggested. ("Thank you for that contribution, Jordan. It is useful for all of us to keep in mind that not everyone will respond positively to Project X.")

The facilitator is a juggler. He or she should be able to manage multiple conversations, off-topic discussions, sarcasm, excessive joking, insults and comments as well as making sure the meeting gets its work done. He or she needs to insure good meeting discipline is followed or the meeting may devolve into a bull session or a "blame storming" session.

Facilitation is a key ingredient to successful meetings. While the senior person present usually runs the meeting, sometimes there may be a better choice. Most meetings benefit from having someone in charge with facilitation skills. You want someone who can get everyone comfortable with contributing. You also want someone who can shut participants off, tactfully, when they talk too much.

Marc Archambault wrote in a blog entry, "Some meeting leaders want to avoid being seen as the heavy by shutting someone down. In reality, everyone else in the meeting is wishing the facilitator would rein in the person that is going on and on. A good facilitator can rein them in without shutting them down or minimizing their contributions."

The facilitator's challenge is to get participants to invest themselves into the meeting. Without some amount of buy-in and give-and-take, the meeting will be more like a lecture or a one way communication. This is not good; when people do not participate, they tend to let their attention wander. And most of the benefits of having a diverse group with additional backgrounds and expertise are lost.

Paul Niquette was the Corporate Director for Product Planning at Xerox Corporation for 15 years. He managed more than his fair share of meetings and wrote a book about it *(Sophistication: How to get it...then what!)* He suggests that the sophisticated meeting facilitator or leader performs the following functions:

- Raises comfort levels in all participants
- Reassures people that no solution is perfect, and,
- In place of full agreement, stimulates GNCD (good natured cooperative dissent).

Sensitivity to the group

The chair should be sensitive to the quality of people's energy in the room. If participants start nodding off, a break or some kind of exercise to get people up and moving around can usually improve people's ability to concentrate.

Many things can affect the energy of the group. Time of day is one important factor; right after lunch is usually where many people's energy lags. Not for nothing is it a time for siesta in many other countries. Late in the day, after people have put in many hours of work, they also tend to lag, and meetings held at such times may suffer from an inability of the participants to focus. Meetings held immediately after any taxing activity – whether physically, mentally or emotionally taxing – will also tend to lag. Reschedule, or rearrange the planned discussion so that they are brief and to the point.

Characteristics of the room can influence people's attention span. If the room is hot, and it is after lunch, watch out! While it is a rule of meetings that the more comfortable the room, the longer the meeting, you want to calibrate the meeting to the room (or vice versa). If you find people squirming around and having trouble sitting still, either the topic is disturbing or the meeting has gone on too long. Or perhaps it is merely that the chairs are uncomfortable.

Action Planning

If action is the hoped-for outcome of a meeting, then planning for action is an important part the meeting. So many meetings, even good ones, conclude without setting up any actionable items, which greatly increases the chances that you'll need to hold the same meeting over again. Action planning consists of defining tasks, establishing who is responsible for those tasks, and creating timelines for completion of particular steps in the action. These are necessary steps to make sure the proposed action actually gets taken.

Without such planning and assignment of accountability, and without creating a structure which lets people know what they need to do and by when, as well as what they can count on for others to do, no complex task will go to completion. The more likely outcome of a failure to do appropriate action planning is that a few people will move ahead in an uncoordinated way, and that acrimony will develop when the pieces they need to continue moving forward fail to appear.

On the other hand, appropriate action planning is useful, even when it needs occasional tweaking as circumstances change. Action plans that are shared with everyone immediately afterwards – and posted prominently – really help move things along.

With appropriate action to manage the talking part of the meeting and timely preparation work, our facilitator is half way home.

Manage the meeting to the bitter end

As the meeting draws to a close, the energy in the room may begin to drag; people stop making eye contact and their attention begins to wander. More side-conversations spring up, and people become careless with meeting etiquette as cues that they are beginning to shift their focus to the next part of their day: lunch, more tasks, or the drive home.

Before the meeting breaks up, the facilitator should summarize decisions and future plans. The team leader or another participant should summarize what was decided and where the project is. This is also the time to make sure each item in the agenda was covered. When everyone is eager to get going, it is all too easy to let something slide. So make sure part of the meeting checklist is to have either the Chair or the note taker run through the agenda making sure everything has either been covered or formally shifted onto a committee or a future agenda. This catches many oversights that might be missed otherwise. There may be areas of discussion which need to be tabled, pending further information or more time for exploration. Meeting participants need to formally agree on a future date to cover these topics, or agree they no longer need coverage.

Chapter 9

Facilitating the
problem-solving
meeting

Root Cause Analysis is a process for following the causes of an adverse event back in time to understand the factors that led to a disaster. Sometimes after a disaster people rush to point fingers and allocate blame without understanding the many factors that may have created the problem. ("Humpty wouldn't have fallen and died if there was a safety rail on the wall. You should have put a safety rail up there!")

Slapping a bandage on the surface of the problem usually means the underlying factors which led to the problem are never addressed, and the disaster may be repeated. The Root Cause Analysis method can be used to keep tracing causes and contributing factors back until you have a good enough grasp of what happened that you can intervene to stop a repeat future event from happening. (Humpty was drunk before he climbed up the wall. Not only a safety rail, but a breathalyzer might be necessary. A quicker response by 911 could also have helped. Perhaps it is also time to upgrade the local hospital to a Level III Trauma Center.) The process of tracing back the series of events and turning them into various types of displays and narratives usually takes place at specialized problem solving meetings.

A problem-solving meeting is more focused than other types of meetings. This means a simplified agenda, tighter control over who is invited to participate, and less tolerance for veering off track. But the rewards can be great for a well-run problem-solving meeting, because an effectively facilitated problem solving team is more intelligent than any of its members, and the outcome can be far superior to the work team members would do on their own.

The problem-solving meeting may be more informal, often lacking formal invitations, agendas, etc. Yet they still benefit from facilitation, with someone taking charge of the mission, the minutia, and keeping people on track. Particularly useful for problem-solving meetings are to have someone steering things along in order to:

- Keep the team on task
- Nip blamestorming sessions in the bud
- Make sure everyone has a voice

You will be collecting a good deal of information. To keep the group focused; organize all the information into its appropriate basic information tools (time line, process map, cause tree, etc.).

The facilitator has to have knowledge in and facility with these four common problem solving tools:

- Timeline
- Cause tree or cause map
- Process map
- Pictures, drawings, audio, video and sensory data

Any data collected that does not fall into one of those four tools should be saved in a format that is easy to retrieve. In the beginning of the analysis there is no way to know which piece of evidence will become critical at the later stage.

Teaching the reader how to do Root Cause Analysis is beyond the scope of this book. But for illustrative purposes we have included an information form from the Queensland (Australia) Patient Safety Board given to people being asked to participate in an RCA (Root Cause Analysis) team. The flyer is designed to answer the most common questions of a potential team member. Your team members might have similar questions, so feel free to adopt the format and substitute answers appropriate for your situation.

Root Cause Analysis (RCA) - A Guide for RCA Team Members

You have been asked to be on a RCA Team.

www.health.qld.gov.au/patientsafety/documents/rcaguide.pdf -

This leaflet aims to inform you about the Root Cause Analysis (RCA) process and outlines your responsibilities as a RCA Team Member. It is intended as a guide only. If you would like further information, contact the Patient Safety Centre on 07 3636 9714.

What is a "Reportable Event"?

Reportable events are those events prescribed in the Health and Other Legislation Act 2007 and are described in detail within the Severity Assessment Code (SAC) table on page 17 of the Queensland Health Clinical Incident Management Implementation Standard (CIMIS) 2008.

What is a Root Cause Analysis?

An RCA is a systematic process used to determine:
- What happened?
- Why it happened?; And
- What can be done to prevent recurrence?

What is an RCA Team?

A RCA Team is a group of people appointed by a Commissioning Authority (or approved delegate) to analyze the events that led to a Reportable Event. The Commissioning Authority will appoint people to the RCA team who have the skills, knowledge and experience to conduct a RCA and who were not directly involved in the provision of the health services associated with the event.

Why I have been asked onto the RCA Team?

Your role on the team will generally fall into one of four categories: 1) Content Expert 2) Front-line Worker 3) Technical RCA Expert 4) Personal from an unrelated area, to provide an objective or 'fresh' view.

When is an RCA not appropriate?
RCA is not the appropriate tool for investigating:
- The professional competence of individual clinicians in relation to the reportable event.
- Finding out who is to blame for the happening of the reportable event.
- Investigation of alleged "Blameworthy Acts".

What does an RCA Team do?

The role of the RCA Team is to analyze the event to determine what happened, why it happened and make recommendation to prevent similar events. The RCA team reviews the medical record of the patient, interviews staff and reviews relevant policy, procedure and standards. The team may also conduct site visits to the physical location where the adverse event occurred to gain a better understanding of what and why it happened.

What is a Blameworthy Act?

A Blameworthy Act is:

- an intentional unsafe act;
- deliberate patient abuse; and/or conduct that constitutes a criminal offence.

What protection do I have?

The RCA Team members have protections afforded by Part 4B of the Health Services Act (Qld) 1991 that include:

the identity of team members, protections from liability for acts done or omissions made during the conduct of the RCA and provision of a report to the Commissioning Authority, protection for the giving of information to the Commissioning Authority and protection from acts of reprisal or attempts to cause detriment.

What obligations do I have as a RCA Team member?

- Utilize your skills, knowledge and experience to undertake a thorough analysis of the incident.
- Assist in the preparation of an RCA Report for the Commissioning Authority that contains a description of the event, the factors the team consider to have contributed

to the event and recommendations that will prevent further recurrence of the adverse event.

What if the RCA Team members cannot agree on findings?

- It is normal for differences of opinion to arise during a RCA. It is the job of the RCA Team Leader to manage any disagreement. In most cases, this can be resolved with consensus being reached. In the event of conflict between RCA Team Members, involvement of the Commissioning Authority and/or Patient Safety Centre maybe required.

Can I discuss the RCA with colleagues?

- Strict confidentiality provision exists in relation to RCA information. To avoid inadvertent breach, the RCA team can ONLY give information regarding the reportable event to the Commissioning Authority.

Who pays for my participation as a RCA Team Member?

- RCA Team Members perform this role during working hours. Line Managers are required to facilitate the team member's attendance at schedule meetings and also provide time to conduct a review of documents, complete site visits and interview witnesses.

Why should I take on this role?

- As a member of a RCA Team you have an opportunity to contribute to improved patient safety by assisting Queensland Health learn from adverse events.

- Many RCA Team Members also report a better understanding of the health care system, the work of colleagues and communication. For many, this leads to changes in their own attitudes and practice behaviors.

Focus is key

With problem solving or root cause analysis meetings, the more focused the meeting, the better. Meetings can be time killers if they are not managed. But problem solving meetings are just specialized forms of regular meetings. As you scan the list of recommended ground rules for these specialized meetings, below, note the similarities with ground rules suggested previously for more general meetings:

- When you start up problem solving or RCA meetings, have everyone review these (or your own) ground rules
- Report on the current state of the project's timeline, cause tree, process map and other tools adopted at prior meetings.
- Encourage everyone to participate in the meeting. This is essential since the process depends on all different kinds of contributions. A "crazy" contribution said in jest by one person might stimulate a thought in someone else that contributes to the process or the problem's solution.
- Every participant should come prepared (having read any reports, viewed pictures, completed their assigned task, etc.)
- The facilitator should redirect any side conversations, off-topic discussions, etc.
- Agree to ban texting, tweeting, answering E-mails, taking any phone calls in the room unless related to the topic at

hand (these meetings tend to be short and intense)
- Pay attention to everyone speaking
- Have an open mind (and a closed mouth)
- Be patient and calm
- Summarize decisions and future plans before you leave the meeting, especially action items

Idea for action: *A great resource for RCA team training and software support is www.RCART.com.au*

Evaluation

Patrice L. Spath, an expert in problem solving meetings, reminds teams of the importance of reviewing team processes to help improve the functioning of any problem-solving team. She suggests developing a formal, written process for capturing the RCA team's evaluation comments. Ask the RCA team to document their answers to the following questions:
- What went right? Why?
- What went wrong? Why?
- What contingency plans had to be implemented? Why?
- What totally unexpected events impacted the RCA project?
- Why were they unexpected?
- Could they have been anticipated?
- How could they be anticipated on future projects?
- How well did the RCA model used in this facility guide the project? How could it be improved?
- What advice would you give to a group of people about to undertake a RCA? What would you have done differently?

The following facilitation tips specifically for RCA team meetings have been adapted from Mark Galley, an expert in RCA and facilitator of hundreds of sessions:

- The cause map, time line and process map created by the team is the primary tool for facilitation. Always go back to those if there is any confusion or you get bogged down.
- A simple sketch on paper or a dry erase board immediately provides the group with a picture that everyone can edit, improve, point at and comment on. Don't overlook the importance of a simple sketch.
- When you assign blame, you end up reducing everyone else's accountability. If I blame a worker for not seeing a dim red warning light, then I am not holding myself accountable for a poor design, placement, alarm, etc., of that light. By avoiding blame, you expand accountability to every person and process in that cause tree. This allows many more possibilities for fixing the problem for the future.

Managing contributions to the team:
- If someone insists on their one solution, keep asking them why and record their answers (they might be exhibiting the certainty paradox). This will help create one complete branch and the blamer will (hopefully) relax.
- Any time a person says "the problem is …," or the … is a cause and should be put on the map. Causes that look like "the problem" from one or more points of view are usually legitimate causes, though they may not be the only causative factor to be considered.
- Rule of thumb – Add something to the map (taking 10 seconds) rather than argue over it (taking 10 minutes).

- Do not tell people that their cause is wrong. Just put it on the map, unconnected to anything else, and ask where it fits in.
- People are naturally biased toward the opinions offered by others from their particular field of view.
- Some people tend to blame and can get fixated on their point of view (e.g. Employee X didn't follow a procedure.) They may take a general view of events without seeing the myriad of details and the contributions of all the causes. They may fail to ask the follow up question, "Why did Employee X do that?" By not looking deep enough, they cannot make their solutions stick.

Get'er done!
- In general, the quicker the better; the longer the process takes, the more likely people will tune out.

Tricks and pitfalls to watch out for
Organizations apply a variety of tools to solve problems, improve operations and increase reliability – often without success. Why? More than likely, according to Mark Galley, they make one or a combination of six common errors:

- They focus on blame.
- Conducting root-cause analysis, they focus on finding one single cause, failing to see many other contributing factors (there is rarely a single cause to any event but rather a cascade of events that if any were interrupted the end result would not have happened.

- They consider the problem description and problem analysis to be the same thing. Description is essential but does not substitute for a deep analysis and understanding of the sources of the issue.
- It might seem counter intuitive but the first step of the meeting is to go back to the organization's goals and figure out which ones were broken by the event. Some people want to jump in without setting a context, and start an investigation by trying to find the problem, instead of identifying an organization's goals
- People sometimes apply "buzzwords" such as "employee empowerment was missing" or concepts such as having lazy employees instead of following the basic technique of cause-and-effect. This approach rarely produces useful results.

In problem-solving investigations, be sure to be alert when you hear one of these generalizations:
- human error
- procedure not followed
- equipment failure
- training inadequate
- design flaw

Many groups believe that the end of an investigation has been reached if they can get to one of these five categories. But why did the human error occur, and what can be done to minimize the risk of having such errors come about? Why was the procedure not followed – did the organization fail to train its staff, were there circumstances that made it seem too risky, or what? Why did the equipment fail – too old, not maintained adequately, poor choice of equipment? Don't stop your investigations too early – ask at least two or three more "why" questions to get more specific information. If you fail to follow it through, you will fail to identify the areas that need modification in order to keep the same problems from cropping up again.

Err on the side of simplicity

William of Occam (c. 1285–1349) is attributed with the idea that "the simplest explanation is most likely the correct one." This ancient principle is sometimes called Occam's Razor.

One positive result of including front-line people (workers, not engineers) involved in your problem-solving team is that they will probably prevent the problem solving process from excessive complexity. Sometimes some people make the conversation too theoretical or use jargon to lock others out or control the result (e.g. an IT person who uses computer jargon that most others don't understand.)

Keeping the process simple makes sharing easier. Keeping it simple makes it easier to understand the thinking and the solution. Therefore it will be easier to engage and involve people in being involved in the solution. Simplicity also allows a bigger network of people who can contribute. Always work to remove the fear of looking silly. Once this is removed, sharing is easier.

Chapter 10

Advanced Facilitation

Have you got the main ideas down pat? Ready for additional challenges and techniques? Below are a variety of refinements, advanced techniques, special situations, tips, tricks and traps to keep in mind.

Stuck in the mud

One of the biggest challenges to the status quo in an organization comes about when a new, outside facilitator comes in to take over running a series of meetings. Typically an outsider can walk in and immediately notice where things don't work. They can observe where people are stuck in old models and antiquated techniques, where people act dysfunctionally, where things bog down or rile up in needless conflicts. This outsider's perspective can last for several meetings. This is the best time to intervene to note problems and make improvements. If the organization doesn't act quickly, the value of the outsider's perspective is lost; the new facilitator will often lose the ability to see the entrenched habits and thought processes and become part of the problem themself.

Brainstorming

The term "brainstorming" was popularized by Alex Osborn in the 1953 book Applied Imagination. Osborn, an advertising executive, began developing methods for creative problem solving in the late 1930s. He was frustrated by his employees' inability to develop creative ideas individually for ad campaigns. In response to this, he began hosting group-thinking sessions and discovered a significant improvement in the quality and quantity of ideas produced by employees.

The process caught on because it became obvious to people in many industries how useful it was as an idea generating technique. Widespread as it has become however, people tend to forget to put it into use in the often contentious give and take of ordinary meetings. So even if you are sure you've seen this again and again, take the time to review the section below. This will greatly increase the likelihood that you will remember to suggest brainstorming techniques in your meetings where appropriate.

Instructions for brainstorming
- When an idea is spoken, write it down.
  - Write down exactly what the person says. People often assume they will remember details, but capturing it imme diately leads to far more accurate results.
  - Most people use a flip chart (advantage - you can save the pages) or a whiteboard (even better if it is an electronic one). A computer with an LCD works well too. Using a white board or chalk board is only good for the immediate discussion; if that is all there is, make sure someone cap tures it in some more permanent mode before it gets erased.
- Do not spend time discussing or refining ideas at this point. Just keep the ideas flowing.
  - Don't try to edit or fine-tune at this stage of the process –

such comments may be seen as criticism, and tend to sti fle the flow of ideas.

- Do not give feedback, make comments or evaluate feasi bility. All ideas are good at this stage of the game – if only because they spark additional, possibly better, ideas from others.
- Invite informal, odd, different, easy, and difficult ideas. All kinds of ideas are okay at this stage of the game.
- Encourage people to invite ideas from all the other team members
- Even weird or jokey comments might stimulate another person's great idea

Once the flow of ideas has stopped, that is the time to evaluate feasibility, comment on, and rework the ideas. When you are done with brainstorming, pick a few favorite ideas that seem the most promising and develop them. Keep the original list because if the first things don't pan out, you can work up additional ones.

Alternate method of brainstorming

Working alone, everyone in the group writes down all of their ideas on paper or typed into files. The same rules apply: do not spend time editing or refining ideas, just keep the ideas flowing.

If you are sitting around a table (note that a table can be virtual – you do not actually have to be in the same country, let alone the same room), the second step is to pass your list to the person sitting next to you. They take your list and, based on what you wrote, add anything that occurs to them. The lists are reviewed by everyone around the table. If there is real interest, the lists might go around again until (for now) all the ideas are squeezed out.

After everyone has had a shot at all the lists, the group goes on to the next step.

This process works well for introverts. But it doesn't always offer the synergy of people's ideas sparking other ideas in the same room.

Ten psychological traps that facilitators face

Being human, people tend to justify their ideas and positions, but their efforts to justify them can lead to judgmental behavior, thinking patterns that stay in unproductive ruts, and other patterns that may interfere with the goals of their organization. The good facilitator will train him/herself to listen for any of the following mechanisms being used to justify someone's position at their meetings.

These are the same fallibilities that scientists have to be alert for, in doing their research. The difference is that in science there is a long tradition of checking for these problems, while in nonscientific organizations there is no such safety mechanism. So be on the lookout for these common traps:

1. Dissonance

Why is it often hard to change your mind about a previously made decision? What mechanism keeps a company turning out the same product the same way (prizing consistency), only to be defeated by another organization with a new approach or a tweak on the product design?

The psychological mechanism is called dissonance. Dissonance is a situation where there is a lack of consistency or compatibility between actions and beliefs. Its more common definition is from music, being "a combination of sounds that is unpleasant to listen to." When the gap between actions and beliefs is large enough, the disjunction is extremely unpleasant to people.

Yet this gap may indicate there are new circumstances which make it time to retire previous good decisions which no longer seem appropriate.

The elimination of dissonance is a powerful motivation because dissonance feels bad. It turns out it is also a motivation to cover up problems and mistakes. The cover-up at first seems to eliminate the uncomfortable gap, but it will become increasingly clear that all it does is put a pleasant-looking bandage over a wound that is beginning to rot.

When a problem your team meeting has decided to investigate is based on a mistake or a judgment error, you may be facing dissonance.

2. Rationalization

Rationalization (commonly known as making excuses) is the process of constructing a logical justification for an action, belief or decision. It is a defense mechanism in which perceived controversial behaviors (mistakes of some kind) are explained in a rational or logical manner to avoid the true explanation (the person messed up). Rationalization is a common reaction when people are more afraid of being blamed than they are interested in finding out what happened and what should have happened instead.

One solution to rationalization is to avoid the need for it. Organizations or teams that avoid blaming and support reasonable experimentation tend to suffer much less from rationalization.

3. "Correlation implies causation"

Statistical knowledge is not well distributed in the general population. A statistician would rarely make the mistake that correlation implies. If two facts are correlated, are they related by cause and effect? A recent medical journal stated the results of a very large study that kids who take one or more tablets of Tylenol have twice the incidence of asthma. The news article led with, "Tylenol causes Asthma?" An unsophisticated public might have concluded that the correlation between the pain medication and the breathing disorder implied that taking certain pain meds causes people to develop life-long lung problems.

In fact, correlation should not be used to imply causation. Correlation between two variables does not automatically imply that one causes the other. Coincidence might be involved, or the presence of other factors. In this case, kids who take Tylenol might have more colds and therefore take more Tylenol. Complicating this, there is good research that colds are causally related to asthma. Leaping to the conclusion that A causes B, simply because you often find A and B occurring together, is a very common problem in research when there is a correlation but no proof of causality.

4. "After the fact therefore because of the fact"

This mistake has been so common for so long that it has an ancient Latin phrase describing it, *"Post hoc ergo propter hoc."* The phrase is Latin for "after this, therefore because of this," and requires that one event occur before the other.

The fallacy comes about when people assume that since event X followed Y, then Y must have been caused X. If I change grease in a bearing and the bearing fails, we might be clever and say that the new grease caused the bearing failure. But more likely, the bearing was about to fail and even greasing it in an ordinary maintenance move would not be enough to prevent it from failing. In fact, we need evidence beyond the mere time relationship for proof of causation.

Post hoc fallacies also manifest themselves as a bias towards jumping to conclusions based upon coincidences. Superstition and magical thinking are two more forms of post hoc thinking. When a sick person is treated by a witch doctor or a faith healer and becomes better afterward, superstitious people conclude that the spell or prayer was effective. Since most illnesses will go away on their own eventually, any treatment might seem effective by post hoc thinking. This is why it is important to test proposed remedies carefully, rather than jumping to conclusions based upon anecdotal evidence.

5. Cherry picking

An observer who only sees a selected data set may wrongly conclude that most, or even all, examples are like that. Example: During a political campaign, each side cherry picks the statistics to make their candidate look superior. Yet there may be many other possible statistics that favor the other side, or are neutral between the sides. Cherry picking can be also found in other logical fallacies. For example, the fallacy of anecdotal evidence tends to overlook large amounts of data in favor of whatever smaller items of information are known personally.

6. Name calling

Name calling is a way to substitute emotional arguments for rational arguments. People use name-calling techniques to incite fears or arouse prejudices in order to invoke fear in their audience instead of letting them use rational thought in making decisions. Example: calling someone a "tax and spend liberal" causes an emotional reaction of distaste, even among independent to fairly liberal voters. The resulting emotions and any decisions based on them may be very different from the emotions and decisions those voters would have made otherwise. Name-calling is thus a substitute for rational, fact-based arguments. This technique is popular amongst politicians and 10 year olds.

7. Red herring

A "red herring" is a tactic that seeks to divert the attention of an opponent or a listener by introducing a new, unrelated topic. The best red herrings are ones that people have strong feelings about; thus any mention of the diversionary topic is likely to bring up feelings strong enough to move the focus of conversation away from the original topic. In current U.S. politics (and in many other parts of the world) all you have to do is say "tax increase" or "cut military spending" and you are likely to move people away from rational thought into the domain of the visceral reaction.

8. Fallacy of the single cause

"What was the cause of this?" is a common question from management about a problem at work or from the public after almost any kind of incident. Such language implies that there was only one cause, and once people identify the first culprit, they can stop thinking. Unfortunately the real world is much more complicated, and all too often there are a large number of (possibly interlocking) causes.

For instance, after an incidence of school violence, pundits and the media debate whether it was caused by the shooter's parents, TV violence, stress on students or the accessibility of guns. This is as if there is "a single cause" to anything as complicated as human behavior. A thorough investigation may uncover a neuro-chemical imbalance, dietary mismanagement, bullying at school, poor parent-child communications, a failed system of teacher-counselor-parent communications, and a variety of other factors, all of which contributed to the tragic outcome.

It is a good idea to identify the cause that gives us the most leverage (least effort and largest impact). This may not be the Root Cause, or a sole root cause, but merely the cause we can eliminate or mitigate with the least effort. Finding and eliminating such a cause will thus reduce the risk of the even recurring, but not eliminate the risk. More effective risk reduction techniques will involve searching for a wider range of contributing factors and working to mitigate more than just one.

9. Circular causation

A circular cause is one where the result of the phenomenon is claimed to be its cause. There are many real world examples of circular cause-and-effect (many of them either virtuous or vicious cycles). Where the circular cause is a cycle, it is a complex of events that reinforces itself. A virtuous circle has favorable results, and a vicious circle has detrimental results.

> *Example of a virtuous cycle: More jobs cause more money in people's pockets which increases consumption, which requires more production, and thus more jobs.*
>
> ....
>
> *Example of a vicious cycle: Expectation of an economic downturn causes people to cut back and spend less, which reduces demand, which results in layoffs, which means people have less money to spend, causing economic downturn.*

10. Third-cause fallacy, sometimes called Joint Effect

In this fallacy there two correlated factors and a third, invisible, factor driving both effects. The famous example is that a city's ice cream sales are highest when the rate of drowning in city swimming pools is highest. To conclude that ice cream causes drowning is spurious. In this case the invisible third factor could be a heat wave that was driving both the ice cream sales and the increased use of pools (resulting in more drownings).

Avoid distortions due to lazy thinking

Beyond the logical fallacies discussed above, another category of dangers for decisions made in meetings has to do with incomplete or lazy thinking. People can be lazy, even in their thought processes. This is called cognitive laziness. There are psychological tendencies that often arise during meetings which create unique barriers to good problem solving:

- Jumping to conclusions – This is one of the most common problems the facilitator runs into. The overwhelming tendency is to go directly from a problem to a solution without thinking it through. Jumping to conclusions feels like making quick progress, but it is progress that often has to be done over again after implementing a too-hasty solution. Meetings with open, non-blaming discussions are more likely to avoid this type of distortion and result in useful suggestions for implementation.
- All-or-nothing thinking – Thinking of things in absolute terms like black and white, good-bad, right-wrong, or all, always, never. Few causes are so absolute. All-or-nothing thinking puts blinders on the decision makers, leading to poorly thought out solutions.
- Overgeneralization – Taking isolated cases and using them to make wide generalizations can cause poor decisions. When you hear someone say something like, "all contractors will try to cheat you" or "it's the fault of those Chinese valves because all Chinese valves are junk," it's time to pull back and say, "Really? You may have had a bad experience once or twice, but does that mean it's always that way?"
- Mental filter – Focusing on very specific and minor aspects of a situation instead of looking at a complete picture, may

distort the decisions and any subsequent plans for action. Example: the fact that a sales order was not signed by the correct party, and so the sale was not finalized, may end up pointing a finger at one sales representative, ignoring the fact that the entire system lacks oversight or leadership. Such mental filters tend to pounce on minutia to the exclusion of substantive issues, or scapegoat the first thing that comes up, rather than identifying system-wide or deeper problems. Solutions based on the smaller picture will be Band-Aids at best.

- Disqualifying the positive – Not seeing anything positive in a person or situation due to fear, rivalry, or unfamiliarity with them. When someone regularly shoots down any positive statement about a person or situation, that person's judgment about that situation is suspect. An overall negative attitude may be spotted by statements like "that will never work here."

- Magnification and minimization – Magnification is common in discussions about risk. People distort aspects of a situation by magnifying or minimizing them out of proportion. One subtype of magnification that is common in meetings is catastrophizing – focusing on the worst possible outcome, however unlikely. There may be a benefit to considering the worst possible outcome, but most decisions are better made considering more probable positive and negative ranges of outcomes.

- Labeling – Labeling is a useful mental trick to categorize facts, events and situations. The downside is the tendency to label something and forget to look at the reality of the thing. This tends to confuse the label with the actuality. Example: Asians are good at math. Actuality: many Asians may be good at math, but many particular Asians may not be so good at math, so prospective employers should test the candidate's math skills before hiring them for math-dependent positions.

- Mislabeling involves describing an event with language that is highly colored and emotionally loaded. Example: John is a crook, John is lazy, John is a waste of protoplasm.
- Personalization – In personalization, a person attributes causes to people who in actuality have little or no control in the situation. Example: After a mistaken decision, workers might conclude that managers are stupid and the cause of everything bad. That attitude short circuits their ability to negotiate or even work with management. The giant downside is that this pattern may get applied to everyone in the same group when attributing blame.
- The Certainty Paradox – Did you ever notice that when an expert has identified a problem, they move forward with certainty and velocity? Experts can see subtle patterns that others miss. Think of the master mechanic looking at a machine, a doctor or surgeon looking at a patient. They often move toward a decision with high speed and confidence.

Sometimes people with little expertise will also act confidently about situations, causes, symptoms and problems. Unfortunately there is a natural tendency to defer the true expert, or at least to anyone who acts like they know what they are doing. This is the certainty paradox. Experts are certain, but fools seem certain too. The team needs to be trained to identify certainty and be allowed, even encouraged to challenge it.

Unconscious bias
Bias has a powerful unconscious effect on decision making in

meetings. People are biased about all kinds of things. There are thousands of biases that people have related to their upbringing, family, schooling and other factors. Each person has to come to terms with their own biases.

Bias is not necessarily a bad thing. The thought is that certain biases aid survival. The attachment to security, discounting problems in the future, and being able to evaluate the likelihood of an event by considering your own tribe's experiences all might have been useful for survival in our distant past. Today the same biases may be unnecessary or even dangerous. It is useful to understand where bias comes from and try to mitigate it through various techniques discussed in this section.

There are some biases that might be called part of the wiring of people's minds. These biases are invisible because everyone has them to one degree or another. Psychologist Scott Plous demonstrated in The Psychology of Judgment and Decision Making that many of the decisions we make are based on unconscious bias.

In this section we will investigate a small sampling of these biases that affect the decisions made at meetings. To evaluate the existence of bias we can use statistical experiments. In terms of statistics if we would expect 50% to answer A to a question and we find 80% answering A, then with research we might say there was bias involved.

Bias coming from the language used to describe the problem

Words have emotional impacts that can completely change perception, memory and opinions. In one experiment, students were show a film clip of an automobile accident. Random groupings were asked how fast the cars were going.

The variable in the experiment was the language used by the experimenter about the movie clip. They wanted to see if language impacts memory. The experimenter used different verbs with different groups of students. Some of the verbs had added zip (e.g. "smashed") and others lessened the emotional load (e.g. "bump"). Here were the results:

Verb used	Mean speed reported by students
Smashed	40.8 MPH
Collided	39.3
Bumped	38.1
Hit	34.0
Contacted	31.8

So the words used had an effect on the judgment of the students up to 25% of their estimates.

A week later the students were asked if they saw broken glass. Based on the verb used to describe the accident the students reported:

Broken glass	Smashed	Hit	Control
YES	16	7	6
NO	34	43	44

When the stronger verb "smashed" was used, more of the students remembered broken glass, although there was none in the original film clip.

Application to meetings:

To some extent our memories are directly influenced by the words we use to recall them. When people report on situations at meetings, be very careful to notice the words that they use. Some words have a strong charge and will create images beyond what actually occurred.

Risk-seeking bias vs. security-seeking bias

Risk management is one of the most important topics discussed at meetings. Which risks people perceive are related to their background, education and attitudes. People who are used to cigarette smoking behavior in their families may live in denial of the risk of lung cancer. Yet a sibling growing up in the same family may go on to campaign against smoking in public places. People who have experienced actual hunger may notice food shortages where people coming from more comfortable backgrounds may notice nothing at all. People who have been through natural disasters may worry about potential threats to life and property in situations where others may breeze through.

This kind of burned-once fear is the basis of the entire insurance industry. Some folks are willing to pay certain known costs up front (insurance premiums) to reduce their risk of losing a big, unknown sum of money in the event of catastrophe (fire, accidents, health problems, loss of life or limb).

Monetary situations are especially conducive to security-seeking behavior such as purchasing insurance to reduce the risk of potential large losses. Non-monetary situations may be more likely to be thought of in emotional terms, including assumptions of luck, invulnerability, and denial of well-documented risks. Take, for example, teenage driving under the influence of alcohol. Many teens will insist, if challenged, that they are good drivers and not really very drunk. The results may not be pretty.

Given a choice, many people would rather gamble on risking a negative outcome rather than take a certain loss. They would push out of their minds a low-probability loss (violent crash) if they had to pay a small price (loss of social "cool") as their other alternative. To test this, researchers asked people which choice they would prefer in a hypothetical gambling situation. Gambling itself may be subject to these same emotional biases, even when it is gambling for money, as so many other factors such as other people's perceptions of you come into play. Answer questions 1 and 2 below for yourself and then read the explanation.

1. Which alternative do you prefer?
A: 100% chance of losing $50

B: A 25% chance of losing $200 and a 75% chance of losing nothing.

2. Which alternative do you prefer?
A. 100% chance to lose $5

B. 1 in 1000 chance to lose $5000

In both cases 80% of people prefer B to A. The problem with that is, statistically speaking, outcomes A and B are identical so you would expect half the people to choose A and the other half to choose B. Since they didn't, the researchers searched for an answer. After hundreds of experiments they found that more people are willing to risk taking big losses in the future rather than take the hit now.

Application to meetings:
If you are discussion a future risk, most people will discount the value and prefer to take the gamble. Most people are risk-seeking when it comes to future losses; they prefer to gamble that they may be lucky enough or capable enough to escape a large loss rather than go ahead and take a certain, smaller loss.

Risk 2 Here is where human the bias for security is clear. Which alternative do you prefer?

A. Paying an insurance premium of $5 that covers the loss from a 1 in 1000 odds on a $5000 loss event.

B. Accepting a 1 in 1000 chance of losing $5000

Findings:

The two alternatives are identical from a statistical expectation point of view. But now there is a reversal of risky behavior when the small amount is being discussed as an insurance premium. Most people have been trained about the benefits of insurance, and so they opt for the insurance! This seems to contradict the first set of choices. But if the problem is framed correctly most people opt for the security. Otherwise very few people would buy insurance.

Application to meetings:

There is a strong bias to "accept" risks of bad events happening (particularly if the probability is small). But people like security and are willing to go for insurance if it is properly priced. If you want people to deal with the risk instead of living with denial of the chance of getting hit in a big way, frame the discussion in terms of insurance policies.

Many experiments have demonstrated these unconscious biases when it comes to risk, reward, gain and loss. The point is to realize that our judgment is shaped sometimes by invisible forces and we should be alert in our meetings if the bias toward security or some other bias is at play.

Hot and cold streaks

This is one of the deepest of the ingrained biases. It drives gamblers to lose money (and provides a very nice income for casinos).

If you had an unbiased coin and flipped it 7 times and it came up heads and you were going to bet $1000 on the outcome of the next flip would you say heads or tails?

    A. HEADS

    B. TAILS

Findings:

Most people feel that the next flip will come up as tails to make up for all the heads that were thrown. In fact each flip is completely independent so the chance of a heads or tails is still 50/50. They confuse the probability of tossing 8 heads in a row (1 /28) from the probability of the next throw being a head (1 /21). These are really two entirely different problems.

Frequently random sequences will have long runs of the same flip and still be random. Most people think random flips will swing back and forth pretty often.

Application to meetings:

In random events the past is no indication of the future. Just because something randomly happened does not predict anything for the future. This same applies to gambling. Good or bad streaks are very difficult to walk away from but the outcome of the next event doesn't know about or care about the past.

Information availability effect

Which is more likely to kill you in the USA today – a shark attack or falling parts from an airplane?

    A. Jaws and his friends (SHARKS)

    B. Airplane parts

Findings:

Most people think shark attacks because information about them is more likely to be in the news or otherwise available to you. In fact you are 30 times more likely to get killed by falling airplane parts. In this case the availability of news anecdotes is grossly misleading

Application to meetings:

If you are trying to make a decision about an unknown that no one has heard of, the tendency is to discount any outcome that none of you have ever heard of. When there is little or no information, don't assume you know the outcome. Just because you never heard of an event happening does not mean it never happens. Common dangers might be under-rated while obscure risks that get a lot of press might be over-rated.

The problem of conjunctive probability

This is one of the most common misconceptions in business. The reason might be related to the fact that most people do not understand basic probability theory. It is difficult to quickly evaluate the chances of something happening if the phenomena depends on several things going wrong (or right).

Suppose you were assigned to build a very complicated machine. Suppose the machine has 500 parts or subsystems that each had a 99% chance of working on the first try. What is the chance the whole machine will work on its first try?

    A. 50%

    B. 10%

    C. 90%

    D. Less than 1%

What did you guess? A and C are the most common guesses, but the actual answer is D.

Findings to meetings:
It seems to be difficult for people to estimate the chances of something happening when there are a string of independent events. In this case the answer is that there is a 1% chance the machine will work on start-up. Each part or subsystem has a 99% probability of working, and all 500 of those parts have to work for the entire machine to work. Assuming each of these probabilities is independent of the others, the formula for calculating the probability of working on the first try is 0.99 * 0.99 * (0.99 multiplied 498 more times), which is quite a bit less than 1%.

Application:
If the meeting is trying to guess at the outcome of a complicated situation, be very cautious about the decisions that follow. This is especially so if you are ball-parking an estimate where there are several independent factors contributing to the end result. The tendency is to underestimate in those circumstances. The recommendations to reduce bias include:
- Keeping good records so you know, for example, how often a failure occurs
- Beware of the tendency toward wishful thinking
- Break the problem up into discrete blocks and evaluate them separately

Anchoring
Why is it that when you are looking for a house, many realtors start by showing you a house that is clearly out of your price range? They explain it as "Oh I know this is out of your range but

I wanted you to see the market." Or, if you are haggling with a street vendor, their opening price is always higher than is credible? The answer is anchoring, a term describing the process of setting up an expectation in a range that the person wants you to be in. For example:

How thick would a giant piece of paper (.003" thick) be if you could fold it in half 100 times?

    A. 1 foot
    B. 1 yard
    C. 1 mile
    D. More

Findings:

People seem to anchor to the first estimate they think of or the first number they hear. That is why a realtor will try to show you a house above your price range. This anchors you upward. In the same fashion, while haggling for souvenirs you should always come back with a ridiculously low number to anchor the seller downwards.

In this case the first few folds of paper 0.003" thick usually anchor people downward. People are usually wildly off. The correct answer is 1.27×1023 kilometers.

Application to meetings:

Whatever number you start with will influence where you think you will end up even if that number is pulled out of the air. Be careful because even people in the know seem to be unable to avoid the effects of anchoring.

Confluence

Confluence is the psychological situation where people sub-merge or hold back their personality to "go with the flow" and not make waves with a dominate personality. Some strong leaders will steamroll everyone to go with (their) program. Eventually they get everyone on board (even if the participant disagrees!) and the meeting gets smoother at the expense of the participants' freedom, self-expression and sometimes their well-being.

Confluence is a description of passivity of the participants and a domineering approach from the chair. While some confluence is essential to the smooth running of the meeting too much will force disagreements underground and could cause passive aggression, back stabbing or unnecessary grumbling. In the worst case conflu-ence will cause people to act against their morals or even the law.

In conclusion –humans are complicated!

We have uncovered a large number of traps and tricks to keep in mind in running meetings. Do not be discouraged by it all. Do your best and keep learning and improving. Feel free to come back to this section of the book again and again. There is always more to learn!

Chapter 11

*Destructive Meeting
Symptoms*

Meetings are made up of people and people are sometimes destructive or pathological. We have assumed to this point that when people assemble for a meeting they share some amount of good will toward each other and toward the task assigned. That is not always the case.

In this chapter we will explore the dark or sinister side of what can go on inside meetings. We can't lose sight of the fact that some people have mental blocks that they trip over when trying to work with others. These blocks or patterns may affect the other participants, who may themselves have dysfunctional blocks or patterns. All this may result in developing actual meeting disorders, which we have taken the liberty of characterizing based on similar psychological disorders found in individual people.

The American Psychiatric Association is a psychological body among whose tasks are to name and describe all types of human psychopathology. Their manual is revised every so often and the 5th edition, the DSM-5, is soon to be published. We will use that as a guide to what can go wrong with people in meetings. In fact certain meetings themselves seem to take on the pathology of some of their dominant participants.

We are using their disorder names (taken from the DSM-4, still in force as of this writing) to describe a set of observable symptoms that you may come in contact with. These labels are not generally used in the field but are instructive nevertheless.

All these disorders can be acute (usually precipitated by some event) or chronic (ongoing for a long time) and can be intermittent or constant. As with all disorders, when they are mild, they are within the range of normal behavior. For example the first category disorganized meeting disorder is the severe end of the spectrum that spans from just a little disorganized all the way to a pathologically disorganized meeting.

The primary barometer of a meeting that might be pathological is the feeling of frustration, wasted time, fatigue, and general malaise. Of course there are disorders that psychologists call ego syntonic which means that the person creating the problem does not appear to suffer from the disorder.

Disorganized meeting disorder

This is probably the most common disorder. Many meeting structures (such as the agenda and minutes) are designed to mitigate the normal amount of disorganization found in groups of people. Disorganization becomes a disorder when it actively interferes with the business of the meeting and produces intense feelings of frustration among the participants.

Disorganized meeting disorder is characterized by lack of agenda (and if there is an agenda, an inability to find it), discussions that wander and cover the same material sometimes several times, disagreements of decisions made at previous meetings and several conversations going on at the same time.

Most of the time this disorder is sourced from the chair or facilitator. There could be a variety of reasons for this including sickness, extreme preoccupation, senility or someone who has a strong aversion to being in control.

Avoidant Meeting Disorder

This disorder comes about when the people leading the meeting refuse to discuss a big but unacknowledged issue (like the proverbial 800 pound gorilla in the room). This is parallel to the psychological disorder of a person who avoids others because of a deeply ingrained fear of being ridiculed, humiliated, rejected, or disliked. If you find that avoidance of issues in your meetings is a common problem, your meeting might be suffering from Avoidant Meeting Disorder.

Symptoms to look for:
- Hypersensitivity to rejection/criticism
- Cutting off discussion when it gets close to forbidden areas
- Inability to face emerging situations
- Self-imposed social isolation (resistance to inviting others)
- Feelings of inadequacy and severe low self-esteem
- Mistrust of others (outsiders)
- Emotional distancing related to intimacy
- Highly self-conscious
- Self-critical about their problems relating to others
- Problems in occupational functioning

Delusional Meeting Disorder

Some people seem like they are not living in the real world.

Occasionally it is because they are visionary. At other times it is because they are delusional. When a meeting is characterized by situations which could be true but are not, or are greatly exaggerated, you might be suffering from delusional meeting disorder. This would include feelings of being spied upon, followed, deceived or conspired against. The delusions are not entirely bizarre (possible but not probable) but seem exaggerated based on real-world evidence. This delusional disorder can be subtyped into the following categories: grandiose, persecutory (most common), somatic, and mixed.

Narcissistic Meeting Disorder

In our everyday lives we interact with people for whom everything is about them. While this might be a minor problem in regular social or business interactions, it can be a huge problem in meetings. Meetings, by definition, require the participants to be able to see and work beyond themselves.

The symptoms of narcissistic disorder revolve around individuals displaying a pattern of grandiosity, need for admiration, and sense of entitlement. Often the individual feels overly important and will exaggerate achievements and will accept, and often demand, praise and admiration despite a lack of worthy achievements.

These symptoms, however, may be a result of an underlying sense of inferiority and are often seen as overcompensation. Because of this, such people can be envious and even angry at others who receive more respect or attention, or otherwise steal away the spotlight.

Other disorderly behavior in meetings

In addition to defects in the meeting itself we are also subject to the pathologies of all of the participants individually. So the meeting may suffer from angry, paranoid, passive, aggressive or passive-aggressive personalities, as well as from people working outside their normal range of behavior (tired, cranky, sick, upset, etc.).

Chapter 12

Where to go
from here

How to improve your meeting process

In the section about facilitation of the problem solving meetings we provided a list of questions to clarify the problem-solving process. Similar analysis can be used for all meetings with slight changes in wording in order to evaluate each meeting afterwards with the intent of improving future meetings. Patrice Spath suggests developing a formal, written process for capturing the team's sense of what worked well and what did not. You can do this easily by asking the team to answer some of the following questions:

- What went right during the meeting today? Why?
- What went wrong? Why?
- What totally unexpected events impacted the meeting?
  - Why were they unexpected?
  - Could they have been anticipated?
  - How can such events be anticipated in future meetings?
  - What contingency plans had to be implemented? Why?
- What would you have done differently?

When you start following this process, it may seem uncomfortable at first. Some may feel awkward at asking for feedback, particularly if the questions are addressed to younger or lower-status colleagues. But getting feedback from the people most intimately involved in the meetings can be invaluable for improving the process. Remember the leverage effect; even a small improvement will positively affect many people. Just take a deep breath and do it. You will see your meetings transform from drudgery to an arena for training, development and the creation of a stronger sense of commitment. At the very least, the time spent will be shorter and designed more appropriately to the task at hand.

QUICK QUIZ:

Do the discussions go off-topic regularly?

Do they serve the mission/company well?

Are problems dealt with in the meeting or are they avoided?

How do you feel afterwards?

Meeting quizzes

Another tool is to design a quick meeting quiz. The example below can help identify areas to look into. You can use your own questions or change the questions to study particular issues. Take seriously whatever feedback you get. Yes, there may be one or two comments which come out of an immediate frustration or desire for petty revenge. But there may also be some truth which might be worth addressing for the good of all.

Penn State University has done significant work in improving its meeting culture. They have excellent resources on their web site (see Bibliography). If you want to check out your meeting muscles, take the following more detailed quiz. Ask yourself or your team the following:

Meeting Evaluation Questionnaire

Prep work for the meeting
- Was the purpose of the meeting clear?
- Did the setup of the room help or hinder the meeting process and could it be improved?
- Did the agenda reflect the true business of this group?

Meeting Process
- Did the meeting follow the agenda?
- Did people come late, come and go, or leave early?
- Did the group use conflict in a positive way to differentiate ideas?
- Did the group work toward consensus?
- Was jumping to conclusions allowed?
- Did the team leader intervene when the process seemed ineffective?
- Did the group insist on action commitments (what is to be done, by when and who)?
- How did you feel when you left the meeting (excited, sleepy, raring to get to work, headachy, etc.)?

Afterwards and follow-up
- Did minutes come out in a short time?
- Did they reflect what you remembered from the meeting?
- Was the action plan published and was it clear who was to do what by when?

Ideas for action:

- *Fill in this (or your own) questionnaire. Tabulate it for a couple of meetings. See how you perform and where you can improve.*
- *After several meetings are reported, have a meta-meeting (meeting about the meeting process) to see if changes are needed or even desired. Consider adding data generated by Meeting Defender.*
- *As a result of that work, discuss one item from the Good Meetings checklist in the appendix and decide whether to incorporate it in future meetings. It might seem crazy to meet just to discuss meetings (but get over it!)*

Be sure to follow the good meeting rules outlined in this book.

The neuroscience of meetings

Dr. Ellen Weber is a researcher in brain studies (neuroscience) who has written extensively about meetings and brainpower. She publishes a quiz in her blog (reference in bibliography) that helps people look at the effect of meetings on higher order thinking and well-being. Some of her thoughts:

Challenge: One of the symptoms of a meeting that does not stimulate people to exercise their brains is boredom. Are your meetings boring? Are people excited to come to the meeting? Are your meetings focused?

Emotional tenor: Many of the questions concern the tenor of the meeting – is it a venting session, a bull session, or are people motivated to bring up and solve problems? If you reflect back on several meetings, is the emotional theme a negative emotion such as fear, anger or jealousy? Is bullying allowed? Are meetings stressful?

Training and development: What is the attitude toward new skills and approaches, particularly when facing problems? Is professional development a part of the meeting mix? Is encouragement used to support your people's growth? This is a tough one – would most consider themselves eager and smarter because of meetings?

Creativity: Creativity is a sometimes fragile state of mind. When people are creative, are they met with cynical mindsets that block creativity, rob talent, or stamp out innovation? Another way she puts this is, "Does the old guard kill incentives and adhere to tired traditions?" Do discussions fall into ruts or routines with few chances for change?

Facilitation and leadership: Who does the talking? Do your managers and leaders talk more or listen more? Do your leaders inspire creativity and invention through meeting interactions?

Relationships: Are relationships tense; is trust lacking? Do participants speak about others in thoughtful and generous ways?

Diversity: Is diversity valued? Are women and men's brains valued intellectually in ways that optimize talents? Do different worker groups each get respect?

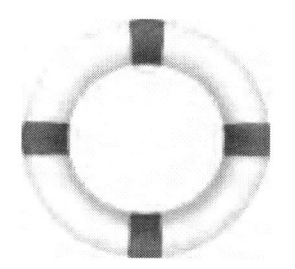

Your present meeting culture

Accept reality. Whatever your organization is doing now is at least partially successful (or better). We know that because (fill in the blank) _____ is being shipped, _____ are being educated, or people are going out the door of your store with _____. In other words even with terrible meetings your company still sells securities, makes bread, transports students, gives out grants or somehow provides some good or service which others value.

In short, as bad as you feel the present meeting culture is, your organization delivers something – it does already, at least somewhat, work.

Still, improvements are possible, maybe highly desirable. To change the meetings culture, the first question to ask is: ***Where are we today?***

Cultural change can be a long journey, and it is helpful to know where you are starting from. In fact, it might be essential. The questionnaires in the previous chapter can help you define your current organizational culture on a qualitative level. In the next chapter we will discuss a tool to help you gather numerical data about your current culture on a quantitative level.

The second step is to know where you want to go.

Ideas for action: Write a paragraph about how meetings are conducted in the proposed new reality (which you get to make up), what it feels like being in them, how actions are carried out and what growth happens to the participants.

In fact, you might want to call a meeting for this!

The third step is to **plan a route.** If you decide to take the trip to better meetings, there are certain places you would want to visit, even places you would like to stay for a while. The important thing is to stay on the journey, keep people reading, studying and whenever possible send people to classes. We encourage you to use the 10 Minutes a Week to Great Meetings feature supplemented by readings in this book as well as using outside classes and resources.

Do you ever really arrive? Probably not, but you can keep getting closer. You can create an organizational culture where the meetings feature excitement, contribution and good will among the participants.

The process will have bumps along the way

What if you try to change your meeting culture and it doesn't go well? This may be time to talk through the problem, study your best practices already in place and consult inside or outside experts.

One of the definitions of maturity is the ability to deal with resistance to change in flexible ways. Some people need more time, others need more logic, and still others need to know what is in it for them. This flexibility allows you to motivate a wider range of people successfully.

- Throughout the process, listen for ideas to resolve any resistance that becomes apparent while still letting both sides save face.

- Own the cultural problem if it's appropriate. If you (in a past or even present job) were a leader in the old culture, acknowledge the facts and explain your motivation for the proposed change.
- Focus on the specifics of the change. Don't dredge up the long history unless it is relevant.
- Change can be frightening. People might try to dump their excess emotional junk onto you because you're a leader. Listen deeply but don't take it in. The tirade is about them and not you!

Changing a culture takes time and fortitude

When you take a close look at the new reality that you invented for your meetings and compare it to your present meetings, one thing should become evident. There will be a gap between what you want and what is. Don't feel bad about uncovering this gap. A wise person once said, "All progress comes from someone who is dissatisfied with the status quo." Nothing will change, and nothing will improve until you realize there is a gap and decide to step across it.

Warning: the first few meetings that occur once you decide to step across will probably be the worst meetings of your career! Take heart; this will be useful in helping you see the gap very clearly.

To make it across you'll need to cultivate three personal attributes:

- **Follow-through** to keep people's eye on the goals. Changes in meeting etiquette and culture will magnify the effectiveness of everything else you do. A common problem in organizations is that when the next big thing comes along, other projects can fall by the wayside and wink out of existence. This may include your own pet project to transform the meeting process. To keep the process on track long enough to do some good, powerful structures and practices have to be invented to remind everyone of what you are doing. Keep promoting the use of meeting checklists, use of previously agreed on meeting etiquette, etc. Your patience will most likely be rewarded.

- **Resilience** to get the process back on track when the program (inevitably) goes off track. If children gave up after they fell, nobody would be walking. The same thing goes for every other skill. It is difficult to get back up on that horse after you fall. To change anything (think about weight, smoking, coffee habits) you just have to keep on getting back on.

- **Positive attitude** – Just as when teaching a child to ride a bike, keep up a positive attitude of encouragement. Don't punish honest mistakes; instead make sure your people are always learning from them. The last thing is to do a check in with people – is it working? Is fun present? If not fix that!

- In addition to these personal attributes it will also help to **develop structures to remind** you that your meetings are great, effective and smart! These structures include such mundane things as being sure the agenda is prepared and distributed, using checklists, putting action items into Outlook with reminders and practices like using ground rules. These structures help organize the process, hold the changes in place, even generating their own constituencies who will remind you if you forget to maintain them – all good stuff!

Another process to create great meetings

Steps

1 Pick your own National Meeting Week! During the chosen week, have meeting participants fill out one of the questionnaires for subjective input. Collect objective input data using Meeting Defender, the meeting calculator that can track time, co2sts and attendance of your meetings in downloadable form for a spread sheet format.

2 Fill in the report data in Excel, reporting on the quality, quantity and cost of your meetings. Using live meeting data you can find out duration, comings and goings, costs and other measures useful to determine your meeting culture.

3 Actions:

   a. Discuss and adapt the meeting checklist to your situation

   b. Institute the meeting check list for all meetings

   c. Build a meeting Poster and put it into every conference room

   d. Take a simplified curriculum from this book and run a short class in good meetings and go over the ground rules you chose to follow.

   e. Take on one item to explore and implement from the ideas list in the appendix

4 After 3 months measure every meeting for a week using the same tools as before. Use the same Excel template. Write up any conclusions from the changes in the observed metrics – lower average cost of meetings, etc.

5 Keep doing this until you reach a point where the team is satisfied with the meetings.

6 Reanalyze the meetings after a year using the same tools.

Chapter 14

Using Outlook™ to manage your meetings

Outlook™ is an E-mail and calendar management and scheduling tool on almost everyone's desktop (laptop, etc.). It is, by far, the most widely used calendar and E-mail tool in the world. It has many useful features to promote good meeting practices, and if you learn them, you have this tremendous resource at your fingertips, all for free!

Outlook™ supports and automates many of the good meeting ground rules. Some of these ground rules include:

- Reply to meeting requests
- Be sure the location and time are in the meeting request
- Ability to remind people of the meeting
- Communicate lateness to meeting organizer
- Great ability to include attachments-
    - Minutes from last meeting
    - Agenda from this meeting
    - Reminder for action items due
    - Research materials, links to review

In the Outlook™ model there are three elements to a meeting: An organizer, attendees and locations. Each person has specific rights and responsibilities. Attendees can be either required or optional.

The organizer sends out all the invitations and receives the replies.

Process:

- The meeting organizer schedules the meeting and sends all of the participants a meeting request which is delivered to the Inboxes of all of the meeting participants.
- Once the request is in the attendee's Inbox, Outlook recognizes it and puts it there as a "tentative" entry in the attendee's calendar until the attendee has a chance to respond.
- Attendees read the request and respond. A meeting response is sent back to the Inbox of the meeting organizer. Once received, Outlook updates the meeting entry in the organizer's calendar with information about who is coming.

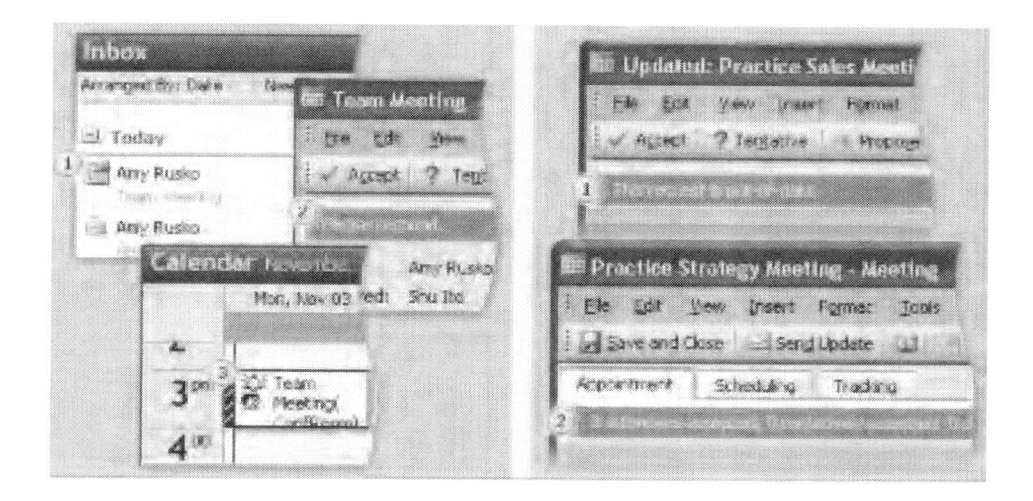

Left Figure: Outlook works behind the scenes to keep up the connections between meeting requests, responses, and entries in your calendar.

1. A meeting request sent to an attendee.
2. The Info bar.
3. A tentative calendar entry for the meeting.

Right Figure: The Info bar in two different meeting requests.

1. The Info bar in a meeting request to an attendee that has been subsequently updated.
2. The Info bar for a meeting in the meeting organizer's calendar, showing a quick count of how many attendees have accepted and how many have declined.

Meeting Organizer

The meeting organizer is in control of the meeting. He or she invites people to the meeting, arranges for a place to meet, and chooses the meeting's time and duration.

The organizer should create a meeting request from the Calendar. Here are three different ways to start the meeting request.

- On the Actions menu, click New Meeting Request. This method gives you a blank slate for the meeting and starts you off in the To box of the meeting request. When you use this method, you'll need to fill in all of the meeting details yourself.
- The second way is to use the "plan a meeting" tab on the actions menu. Use this method when your first goal is to find a time that's free in everyone's schedule.
- Finally you can right-click a selected time in your calendar and click New Meeting Request. You can use this method when you want to book the meeting at a specific time. Because you select the time first, that part of the request will be filled in when it opens.

The meeting organizer sets up the meeting request and controls it in the Calendar. Every request should include three basic details:

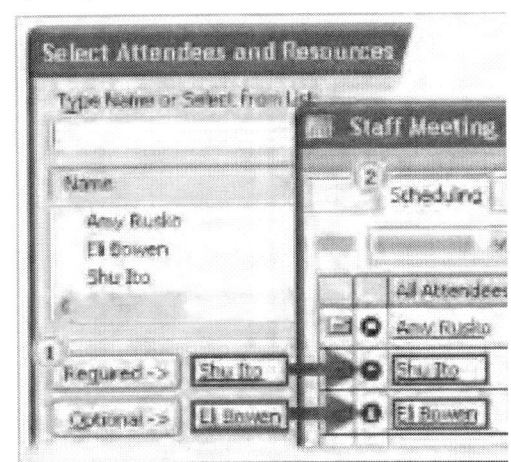

- The people who will attend the meeting
- The time and duration of the meeting
- A place to meet

The Select Attendees and Resources dialog box lets you specify whether an attendee is Required or Optional.

Icons on the Scheduling tab help you keep track of your choices.

You can't have a meeting by yourself (sometimes things would go so much smoother!). A key step in creating your meeting request is to choose the people for your attendee list.

The best way to add attendees to your meeting is to use the Address Book, which you can easily get to from the Select Attendees and Resources dialog box. This dialog box lets you specify whose attendance at the meeting is required and who can opt out.

If you are using Microsoft Exchange Server, Outlook™ can review everyone's calendar and report the time everyone on the attendee list is free. With Microsoft Exchange Server™, people in your organization share information about their schedules automatically. In Outlook™, this information is called free/busy time. The function of the Scheduling tab is to let you check free/busy time for all of your meeting participants, all at once.

Location

Filling in the Location box of the meeting request, you let everyone know where your meeting will be located. How you fill in the location for the meeting request will depend on how things are done at your company. Again the process of reserving conference rooms can be managed by the Exchange server™.

If your company doesn't use Microsoft Exchange Server™ to handle conference room scheduling, you can specify a location for your meeting by simply typing the location of the meeting into the Location box of the Meeting Request. Remember that you may first need to check with an administrative assistant or write your name on a sign-up sheet outside of the conference room to reserve the room.

Handling RSVP to your meetings

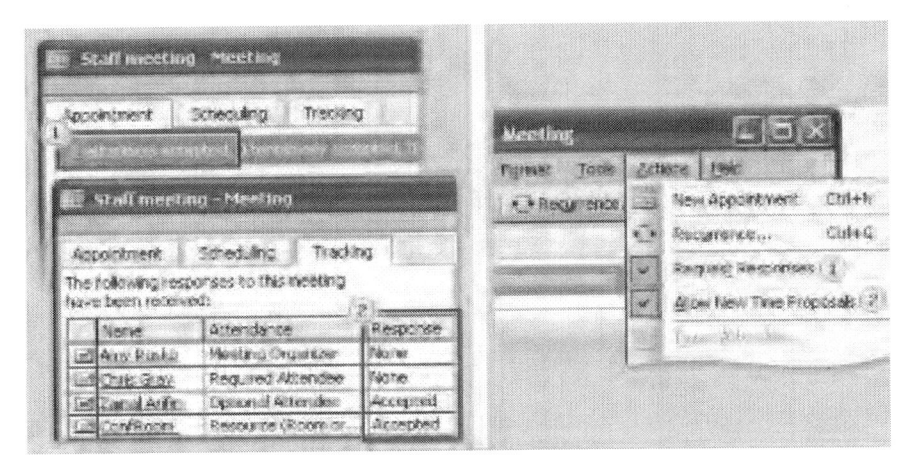

Left Figure: You can track the responses using these tabs.

1. Use the Info bar on the Appointment tab.

2. Look in the Response column on the Tracking tab.

Right Figure: Use these commands to control responses, meeting by meeting. You'll see these commands on the Actions menu when the meeting is open for editing.

1. See responses.

2. Allow others to propose new meeting times.

Once you've set up the meeting in your own calendar, you send the meeting request to the participants by clicking Send.

Track responses

Once you've sent your request and started receiving responses, you can see how many people plan to attend by looking in the Info bar at the top of the meeting request in your calendar (you need to open the request to see this). And you can get more details by looking on the Tracking tab of the meeting item in your calendar.

The following options give you some control over your meeting request:

- Ignore responses: You can choose not to track the attendees' responses. If, for example, you're setting up a meeting for a very large group, you may not want to see all of the responses individually.
- Allow new time proposals: As the one in charge of the meeting, you get to decide whether you allow attendees to suggest new times for your meeting. An attendee who has a schedule conflict may propose a new meeting time in order to make it. For a large meeting, however, this may not be practical.

Attendee (participant) actions

When you're a participant, you need to reply to the meeting organizer, confirming your attendance.

When a meeting request lands in your Inbox, it is automatically added to your Calendar. This reduces the potential for double-bookings and helps you to avoid missing meetings.

To respond to a meeting request, all you need to do is click one of the buttons in the request. When you do this, a meeting response is created and sent to the meeting organizer. Once you respond, the request is removed from your Inbox.

These are your main choices for responses:

✓ *Accept:* Accept a meeting that you know you'll be able to attend. When you accept a meeting, the meeting is scheduled in your Calendar and you receive updates if the meeting organizer changes the details of the meeting. If others view your free/busy time, the time appears as Busy by default.

✓ **_Decline:_** Decline a meeting if you can't go. Declining a meeting deletes the item from your Calendar (freeing that block of time), but it does not sever your ties with the meeting: You'll still get updates if the meeting organizer makes them and you'll have the opportunity to respond to the update. (If you truly want to opt out of a meeting, you may want to ask the organizer to remove your name from the attendee list.)

✓ **_Tentative_** Use this option if you're interested in the meeting, but aren't sure whether you'll be able to make it. The meeting is scheduled in your Calendar and that block of time is displayed to others as tentatively unavailable.

Tips
- Before you respond, read the text in the Info bar to make sure you're responding to the most up-to-date version of the request.
- If you want to check your calendar before you respond to a request, you can click the Calendar button on the Standard toolbar of the request.

Options:
- Include a message with your response Do you need to let the meeting organizer know that you might be late? Maybe you need to verify if lunch will be provided at a lunchtime meeting or whether you need to bring anything to a client presentation. When you respond to a meeting request, you can send a personal note to the organizer. Only the meeting organizer will see your message — it doesn't go to the rest of the attendees.

- It's possible to forward a meeting request to someone else. You should know that when you forward a meeting request, the person you forward it to will respond directly to the meeting organizer. That is, when that attendee responds to the meeting request, the meeting organizer will receive a message directly from that person — you'll be out of the loop.

(This section is based on the excellent on-line training class on organizing meetings using Outlook ™ which can be found at: http://office.microsoft.com/en-us/training/organize-meetings-with-outlook-RZ001166003.aspx)

Chapter 15

Using Meeting Defender software to improve meetings

While in the middle of a meeting not too long ago, I started thinking that an awful lot of salary-hours were being while people sat in badly run meetings fidgeting, texting friends and otherwise losing productive work time. How many dollars were being wasted wouldn't be too hard to calculate if I knew or could guess roughly what people's salaries were. The calculation should include the overhead costs of those hours and possibly even a multiplier for other related costs. How cool it would be, I figured, if we could set up an app that would calculate the waste, and keep on totaling up every additional minute spent in the meeting. You could set it up so that everyone could watch the minutes (dollars) ticking away. When people got too long-winded, other people in the meeting could hold up the screen to encourage them to stop yapping away.

After a few discussions with programmer friends, the idea for Meeting Defender ("Defend the cost of your meetings!" or even "Try to defend the cost of your meetings!") was born.

In beta testing this application, we found that it was not only being used as a fun little gimmick; it also had some good, solid uses for improving meeting productivity. People were using it to monitor the cost of their meetings, then introducing measures for improving meeting productivity. Using our software, they could begin to measure the results of these changes in corporate meeting practices.

 **Meeting Defender Software for Laptops and Desktops can be used to collect data on your meetings**

How to make good use of Meeting Defender

The major components of the software include:
- Meeting Timer
- Meeting Cost Calculator
- Attendance tracking

Meeting Defender times each meeting and keeps track of who was there and when they came and left. It can also keep track of the people-cost of the meeting. When you input the charge rate for each participant or group of participants, Meeting Defender will calculate the salary and overhead costs of the meeting.

Meeting Defender can additionally be used to help you understand aspects of your meeting culture. It can help you answer questions like:
- How long do our meetings average?
- How many people attend?
- Do people come and go during the meetings?
- How much money (direct dollars) do our meetings cost us?
- Does adopting new rules for meetings lead to more produc tive meetings?

How it works

To set up a meeting, you first enter the name of the meeting.

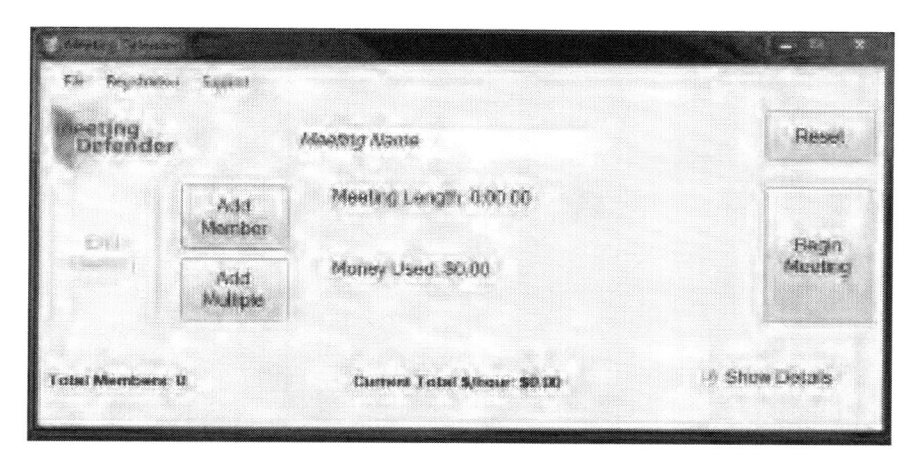

The next step is to add participants. There are two ways to add people to a meeting.

Add one member at a time: When you click the Add Member button you can add someone by name. You may want to include their overall charge rate* instead of just their hourly wage rate (e.g. $55/hour instead of the $25 the employee receives. See discussion below for more details on this issue.

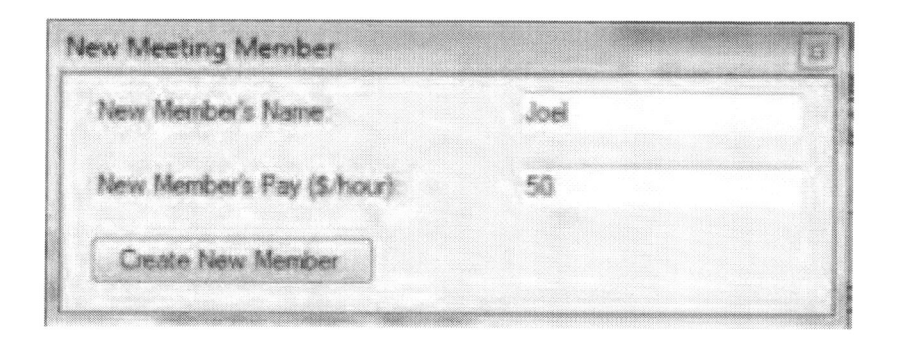

* Let's say a person makes $25 an hour wages. In the US the company has to pay for Medicare, Social Security (FICA), Vacations, Sick pay, Holidays, maybe pension and health insurance. All these things are benefits added to the wage to become the labor cost. Many organizations figure 30% for benefits ($7.50).

Beyond this there are overhead costs for the facility, equipment and supplies where they work (Rent, heat, water, computer, desk space, phone, supervision, etc) These costs are the burden or overhead to have that employee. In different organizations the burden can range from 50% to 200% of the employee's wage rate.

If you add up the wage, benefits and overhead you get the burdened labor rate or what I call it the charge rate. If you don't know your own organization's overhead number, you might use a multiplier of 2.2 (2.2 * hourly wage or in this case $55/ hour) to cover such items as the participant's benefits plus other overhead costs.

Note: *You can add additional members at any time, even after the meeting has started.*

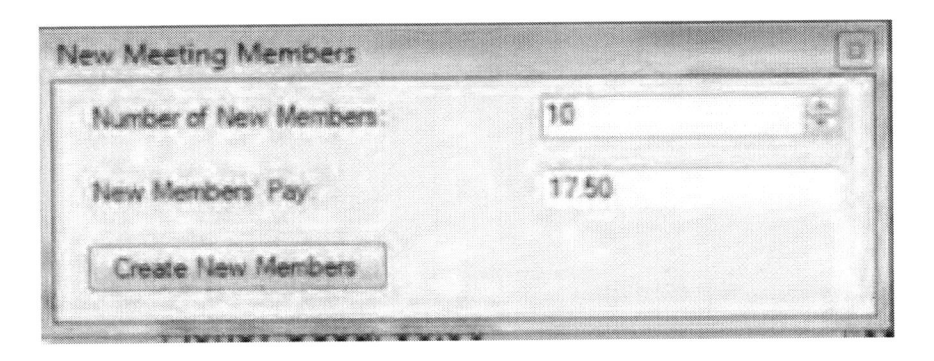

Adding multiple members at a time: (see figure on previous page)When everyone at the meeting has roughly similar wage rates, you can add them wholesale as a group. The screen prompts you to answer how many people are involved and their average wage rate per hour. Again you can decide to use wages or wages loaded with other overhead costs. You can add newcomers to the meeting at any time, even after it has started.

Salary data is frequently confidential so there may be resistance to using actual salary data. There is a good deal of discussion about the wisdom of revealing people's salaries. There are some simple ways to deal with this.

- Have some generic charge rates for different levels of people such as engineer rate, supervisor rate, manager rate, trades person rate, etc.
- Use the same rate for everyone if everyone is generally on the same level.
- Avoid the question by putting in $1.00 for all rates. You will still get an idea of the productivity costs of the meeting simply by calculating the number of person-hours spent in the meeting.

To be most accurate, the dollars wasted should capture the full cost for people in the meeting. So, consider adding benefits, employer side of FICA, indirect time (training, temporary assignments, etc.), and a charge for overhead. For all these charges, many organizations use 2.2 times the hourly salary to cover everything. Nonprofit organizations and various industries may differ greatly in this regard. If you know the multiplier your own organization uses, use that number instead.

Other buttons on Meeting Defender

Reset Meeting: Returns everything to zero, including "Time," "Money Used" and "Members" (removes all participants).

Begin Meeting: When you pull up the program, click here to start the timer and money counter. If there is a meeting already on the display, hitting the start button will restart the previous meeting where you left off. Hit Reset to start monitoring a new meeting.

End Meeting: Until a meeting is running, the End Meeting button is grayed out. During the meeting, click it when the meeting ends. If you want to restart the meeting after a break, click "End Meeting" at the beginning of the break, which will stop the clock but continue to maintain the total so far. Click "Begin Meeting," and the time and money used will start where they left off.

Show Details: Clicking this box shows all the meeting participants and their labor rates.

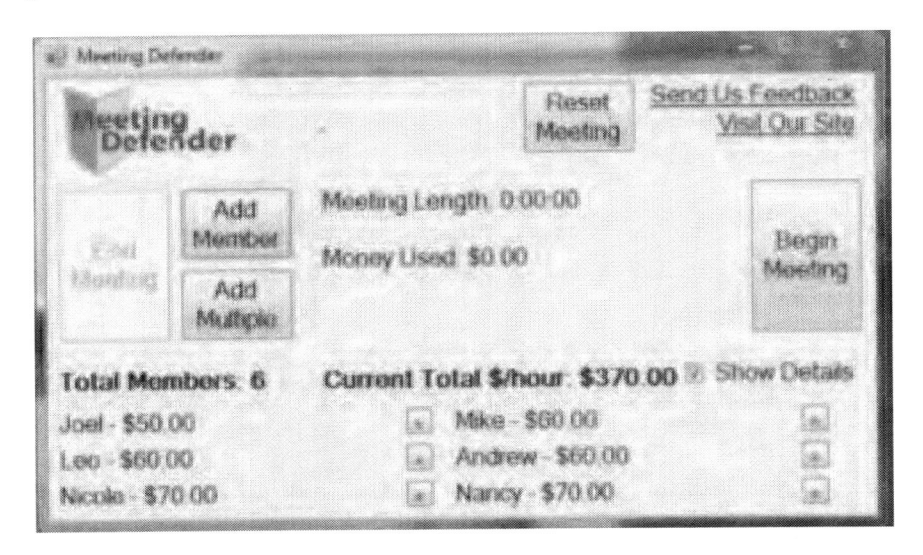

Note: *if you want to keep salary information confidential, do not click this box. Un-clicking the Show Details box shows only the total cost per hour and keeps the wage rates and participants private.*

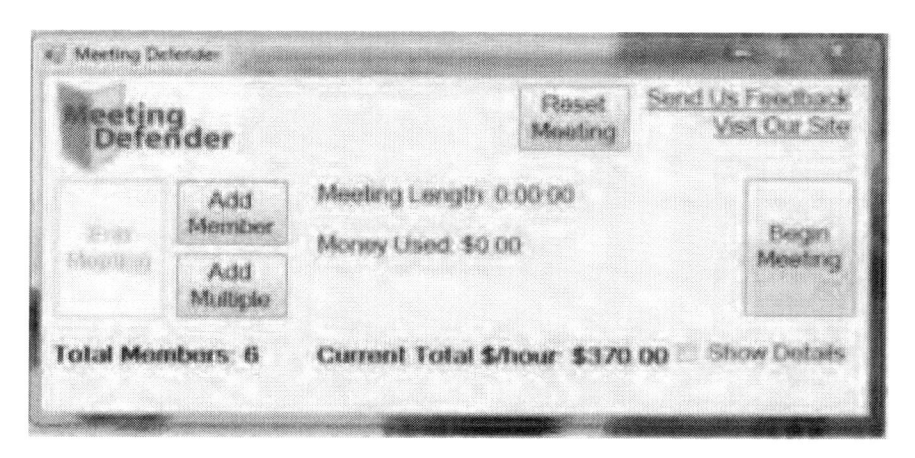

In the image below, the meeting has just begun. Notice the End Meeting button is no longer grayed out. If someone leaves the meeting just click the x to the right of their name and their wages will no longer be added to the current $/hour from that time onwards.

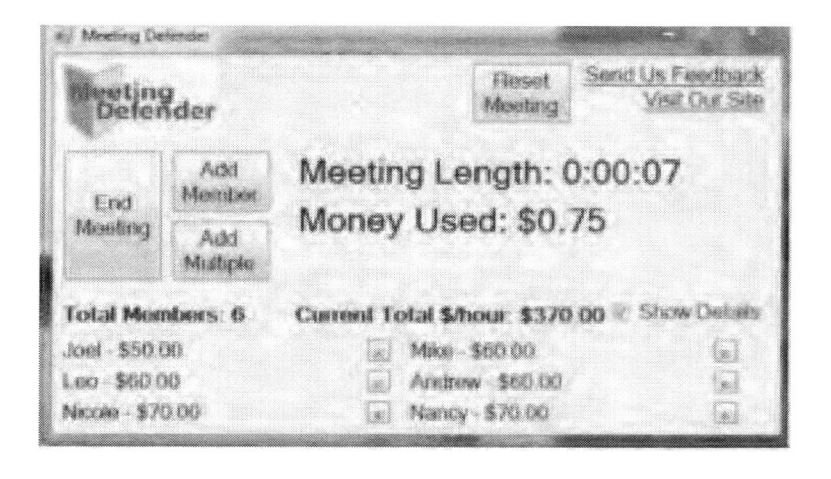

If they return to the meeting later, the person can be added back into the meeting by just clicking the + sign to the right of their name (such as Nicole on previous page).

Deeper analysis available from Meeting Defender

The Meeting Defender program goes beyond simply timing your meetings and calculating their opportunity cost. It can be used to collect statistics about the frequency, length, and number of participants for every meeting it is used in. This information can be used for productivity improvements, meeting training, facilitation and just to give you facts to make intelligent decisions.

When the meeting is over, click "End Meeting" and then click the "Copy to Clipboard" button. All the information including meeting name, participants, attendee arrival times, charge rates, meeting length, and money used will be saved in Excel format. Use this information in other reports, or simply to have as background information.

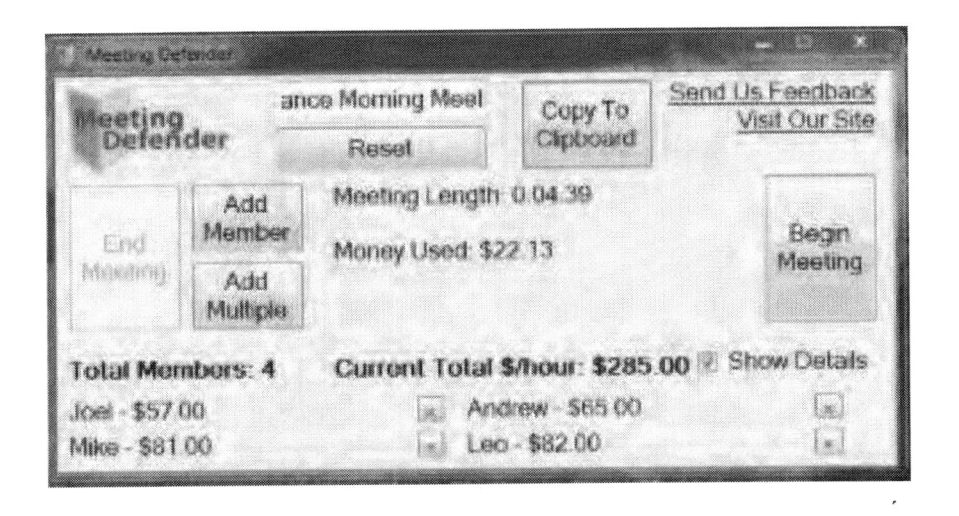

Here is the raw information (tabs added to aid readability) for the meeting:

Meeting Name	"Production-Maintenance Morning Meeting"	
Start Time	**End Time**	**Money Used**
04 Jan 2012 2:57:15 PM	04 Jan 2012 3:01:55 PM	$22.13

MemberPay $/hour		Entered Meeting	Left Meeting
Joel	$57.00	04 Jan 2012 2:57:15 PM	04 Jan 2012 3:01:55 PM
Andrew	$65.00	04 Jan 2012 2:57:15 PM	04 Jan 2012 3:01:55 PM
Mike	$81.00	04 Jan 2012 2:57:15 PM	04Jan 2012 3:01:55 PM
Leo	$82.00	04 Jan 2012 2:57:15 PM	04 Jan 2012 3:01:55 PM

To use the information for any kind of analysis, paste it into an Excel Spreadsheet. As you may note, it is a standard Excel comma delimited or CSV format file.

The "10 Commandments of Meetings"* Poster for Meeting Rooms

1 Thou Shalt Always Know What Time It Is Meetings and organizations run on time. The fuel is time. Be sure you don't waste it. Overtime meetings make for bad decisions.

2 Thou Shalt Not Forget the Main Reason for Meetings People tend to wander off onto whatever else is on their mind. The natural state of group discussions is to wander with them. Meetings are unnatural and need to be kept that way to maintain efficiency.

3 Thou Shalt Remember the Golden Rule of Meetings: Praise in Public, Criticize in Private Any good supervisor or manager knows that people take criticism in very different ways. Many people need time to process it. Without time they might be inclined to attack back. There is no advantage to the meeting in embarrassing someone.

4 Thou Shalt Not Convene Meetings Outside of Normal Business Hours Unless there is an emergency, keep the meetings to working hours. Everyone has work-life balance issues and we don't want to have the person's family resenting the job or organization.

5 Thou Shalt Not Use Group Pressure to Logroll Conclusions Don't use peer pressure to force a decision, especially if the decision is wrong in some way. This will come back to bite you.

6 Thou Shalt Not Use Meetings to Destroy Others' Careers Old adage: "The people you step on on the way up might be the same people greasing the rails on the way down." Treat everyone with respect. There is no doubt you will find yourself needing their cooperation sometime in the future.

7 Thou Shalt Keep the Personal and the Corporate Distinct
Some socializing is good and appropriate before, after and during breaks at meetings. Much more than that becomes self-defeating.

8 Thou Shalt Remember that the Best Model for Meetings Is Democracy, Not Monarchy If you want to tell everyone your decisions, use a video, memo, or some other means. If you call a meeting, the implication is that you want input. If you want input, give people a stake in the meeting; give them some power.

9 Thou Shalt Always Prepare a Clear Agenda and Circulate It Beforehand   An essential element of efficiency and meeting effectiveness. Keeps meeting on track toward a known goal.

10 Thou Shalt Terminate a Regularly Scheduled Meeting When Its Purpose for Being No Longer Exists When the meeting has clearly stated goals it is easier to see if it is no longer needed. Be brave – cancel it. Reviewing a standing meeting against its goals and on-going need should be routine.

*Adapted from the article of the same name printed in the Harvard Business Review.

Do you know the purpose of this meeting?

Is there an agenda?

Do you know your role?

Example of Meeting Management Course Outline from:

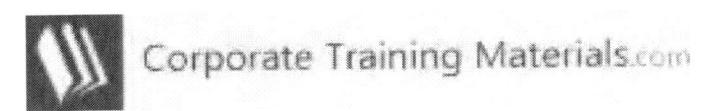

Suitable for larger organizations, Corporate Training Materials is an organization that offers turnkey classes and training materials for your in-house use. This is included below as another resource for understanding the factors that go into organizing good meeting protocol. CTM's course materials include PowerPoints, reference sheets, manuals, and instructor guides.

Module One: Getting Started
- Icebreaker
- Housekeeping Items
- The Parking Lot
- Workshop Objectives

Module Two: Planning and Preparing (I)
- Identifying the Participants
- Choosing the Time and Place
- Creating the Agenda

Module Three: Planning and Preparing (II)
- Gathering Materials
- Sending Invitations
- Making Logistical Arrangements

Module Four: Setting up the Meeting Space
- The Basic Essentials
- The Extra Touches
- Choosing a Physical Arrangement

Module Five: Electronic Options
- Overview of Choices Available
- Things to Consider
- Making a Final Decision

Module Six: Meeting Roles and Responsibilities
- *The Chairperson*
- *The Minute Taker*
- *The Attendees*
- *Variations for Large and Small Meetings*

Module Seven: Chairing a Meeting (I)
- *Getting Off on the Right Foot*
- *The Role of the Agenda*
- *Using a Parking Lot*

Module Eight: Chairing a Meeting (II)
- *Keeping the Meeting on Track*
- *Dealing with Overtime*
- *Holding Participants Accountable*

Module Nine: Dealing with Disruptions
- *Running In and Out*
- *Cell Phone and PDAs Ringing*
- *Off on a Tangent*
- *Personality Conflict*

Module Ten: Taking Minutes
- *What are Minutes?*
- *What Do I Record?*
- *A Take-Home Template*

Module Eleven: Making the Most of Your Meeting
- *The 50 Minute Meeting*
- *Using Games*
- *Giving Prizes*
- *Stuffed Magic*

Module Twelve: Wrapping Up
- *Words from the Wise*
- *Review of Parking Lot*
- *Lessons Learned*
- *Completion of Action Plans and Evaluations*

You can contact CTM at http://corporatetrainingmaterials.com

Good meeting BIG checklist of ideas

The goal of this book is to supply you with ideas to improve your meetings. On the following pages is a compilation the most important areas of meeting management.

If you have problems getting your meetings to become a positive process despite your best efforts, it might pay to investigate bringing in a professional meeting facilitator. There are consultantcies which specialize in facilitation. Within the field there are specialists in formal meetings, non-profit organizational meetings, problem solving meetings and creative type meetings.

✓	Before the first meeting in a series *The good meetings checklist*
	Do you have a document with meeting ground rules that is known and available to participants?
	Design or adopt a quick Meeting Checklist to eliminate recurring problems.
	Before planning the meeting, ask yourself, is a meeting the best way to achieve our goals? Would a memo, email, or poster be more effective?
	If you must meet, would telephone conference, Internet conference or another mode be better?
	Any meeting worth having is worth planning for! Have you done your planning?
	Every meeting needs an explicit goal or goals. What are the goals? Set these goals are at the top of the minutes and agenda to help people keep on track.

✓	**Before the first meeting in a series** *The good meetings checklist*

Have the group name itself. Pick a cool name.

Discuss or decide if you will follow formal rules of order or more informal rules. This choice might be made for you by the type of meeting

Think about confidentiality for this series of meetings. Discuss and periodically remind participants if they opt for confidentiality.

Is the meeting type and timing consistent with the time of day? Consider circadian rhythms.

Have you thought through who should attend? What they would contribute? What is in it for them?

Review the participant list to determine if there is enough diversity of experience, thought processes, background for good discussions. More diversity is useful if the topic is particularly important.

What type of meeting is it? Meeting length is proportional to the comfort of the room (no chairs = short meeting) and to the level of refreshments (add food - add an hour). Keep in mind you might want it comfortable or not, or to serve food or not, to suit your meeting design.

Zero based meeting justification: "(ignoring the issue of tradition)" Can we justify this meeting's time and resource given today's issues and opportunities

✓	**Pre-meeting**
	The good meetings checklist

	Choose an appropriate place for the meeting and manage temperature, sound level and distractions when possible. Reserve the room if necessary.
	Is your agenda finished and distributed with goals, meeting start time and duration, place, attendance, topics and timings?
	Consider putting the most important agenda items second and third on the agenda (not first, to accommodate stragglers and allow people to mentally arrive at the meeting).
	Consider putting times on agenda items. (Example: Discuss problems and decide on a course of action with contractor ABC 15 minutes...). Some leaders only put estimated times on their agenda to guide them. Others use time estimates publicly to help discipline the group's discussion process.
	Tailor the number of agenda items to the type and length of the meeting (and to the attention span of the attendees).
	Invite people to send agenda items to the chair, including any new business.
	Consider reviewing the agenda with your boss ahead of the meeting. This would be particularly useful if there are potentially sensitive or controversial agenda items. Remember the 11th commandment, "Thou shalt not surprise your boss on sensitive issues."
	All handouts (particularly long ones or complex ones) need page numbers, exhibit numbers, tabs and other features to make them quick to navigate and easy to use.

✓	**Pre-meeting** ***The good meetings checklist***
	If there is a PowerPoint were good practices followed in the creation? Did the presenter practice it?
	Give adequate notice for ad hoc meetings (as opposed to regularly scheduled meetings).
	Require meeting participants to do their homework. It helps to remind them before the meeting of their previous agreements. (How do you enforce this? – an organizational question.)
	Andrew's rule: It takes an hour to properly prepare for a 1 hour meeting.
	Share everyone's contact information (can be done at the meeting)
	Decide if any guests are needed. Determine if a particular expertise is needed or a representative from an area is needed (and communicate that fact).
	Have an agreement of terminology, especially if outsiders will be at the meeting. Define all acronyms. The more diverse the group, the more important this is.

✓	**Just before the meeting** *The good meetings checklist*
	Review important presentations ahead of time to avoid surprises. If you are the presenter, consider practicing important presentations ahead of time.
	Have an admin person call everyone on the morning of the meeting (or the afternoon before) to verify attendance (and maybe to remind them of what they promised to do).
	Know who will not attend. Have people contact you when they can't make the meeting (so you don't wait for them). A ground rule is to RSVP to all meetings.
	Check out the AV before the meeting, including any connections to LCD projectors, PPT presentations, etc. You do not want to waste a roomful of people's time fiddling with the equipment.
	Do you know where there is a spare bulb for the LCD or even a whole spare LCD?
	Has your thumb drive been used on the conference room computer? If not, set it up so the driver software will be preloaded.
	Check to see if the room is clean, easel has paper, white board is there, copies have been made, pens and pads, any other aids as needed.
	Decide who will play what roles in the meeting.
	You will be working with the people in the meeting for (hopefully) a long time. If your report to the group embarrasses someone else in the meeting, be sure to give them a heads up before the meeting so they can be ready for it.

✓	**Just before the meeting** *The good meetings checklist*
	Take straw polls (informal polls about where people stand on an issue) on controversial issues before the meeting
	Be sure you have a copy of the prior meeting's minutes with you. Review the last few meetings' minutes before starting the meeting
	Review a copy of the previous meeting's action list which lists all actions promised and dates for delivery.
	Read the mission statement or the goals for the meeting right before you start.
	If people have presentations or reports, verify that they are going to be ready. They do not get to prepare while other people are talking.
	Hard copies of the agenda on hand for reference (including links of where to find any background or support materials required).

✓	**As you start the meeting** *The good meetings checklist*
	Start and end on time. Some companies lock the door after 5 minutes. Some meetings can occasionally run over a little bit but get permission from the team to stay. Note: If meetings are consistently long, the agendas may be too crowded. If you run too long, you have no right to expect people to come to your meeting on time!
	Greet everyone and welcome them to the meeting.

✓	**As you start the meeting** *The good meetings checklist*
	Be sure everyone knows their role in the meeting.
	Have someone take minutes (who is good at it).
	Introduce guests. Be sure contact information makes it into the minutes. Share their role in the meeting.
	Review your ground rules on Day 1 for any new meeting cycle.
	Remind everyone about confidentiality
	Ask everyone to set their phones to vibrate. They should leave the room to take calls not related to the issues being discussed.
	Remind people about text messages, email. Texting, email and web surfing during meetings has become endemic. Decide on some ground rules and (politely) enforce them.
	This would be a good time to review the goals of the group in general and of this meeting in particular with the group. Also a good time to review any ground rules everyone agreed to.
	People come in the door with a variety of concerns and preoccupations. A practice is to start the meeting by asking if anyone has any concerns or worries that may interfere with concentrating on the business at hand
	Ask if meeting goers did their homework. If a critical mass of people have not, immediately cancel the meeting and reschedule.
	Remind people about leverage. An off-topic conversation wastes everyone's time.

✓	**As you start the meeting** *The good meetings checklist*
	Remind people about positive feedback even if they disagree. The appropriate response to anything is "Thank you," not, "This is stupid!" Disagreement is desirable for a complete conversation, but being disagreeable is not.
	Remind people that when decisions are made, they must be formally written into the minutes. All participants must agree to support them even if they did not agree with them during the discussion.
	Build into your discussions the organizational core. This will remind people of the big picture and keep them focused on the same outcomes.
	Have everyone introduce themselves and their role if people don't already know everyone.
	Remind people they are the adventurers or participants, not prisoners of the meeting.
	In meetings of community boards or non-profits the people may only know each other from what they say in the meeting. Either at the start of a meeting or during a break give people the assignment to share some personal information like family, type of work, hobbies, travel, interests, and anything else.

✓	**At The Meeting** *The good meetings check sheet*
	As the leader, be the first speaker and provide a short overview of the meeting agenda.
	If someone is joining the meeting by phone make a name tag to place next to the Conference speaker with the person's name.

✓	**At The Meeting** *The good meetings check sheet*
	When assigning tasks and responsibilities, be sure to include in the minutes who is to carry what out by when. The how and why are useful but not essential. (It is important to create a structure to manage this.)
	(If appropriate to your meeting) Initiate the practice of a safe, sustainability, environmental moment where someone shares something about these topics. Some meetings start and end with safety. (It helps to focus attention).
	Create an environment where people reveal what is going wrong when they speak and what they plan to do about it. They can get help.
	Encourage the practice of looking for failures or weaknesses in your system to be addressed, rather than looking for people to blame.
	Make mistakes into teachable moments. What happened was…, what I learned was…
	As leader, note people who come late. You are not interested in their reasons, just recognize if they realize they were late. If this becomes a habit, have a private conversation with them about the ground rules.
	Practice acknowledging participants' accomplishments.
	Take this a step further: Have everyone in the room share something to acknowledge about someone else in the room – this can turn a divisive moment into a team building exercise.
	To take this a step sideways: Acknowledge someone from another area that has contributed to the work of this group. Make sure they find out that their praises were sung publicly.

✓	**At The Meeting** *The good meetings check sheet*
	No participant can speak twice on the same issue until everyone else wishing to speak has spoken about it.
	Remind everyone to speak clearly and loudly enough to be heard.
	If energy flags, get everyone moving or standing. A good argument will do the same.
	Be prepared to drop a topic that gets stuck and assign it to a problem-solving team which can be a subset of the meeting group,
	Check in with the notes taker and periodically verify they are OK and if they need anything.
	Nip blamestorming sessions in the bud.
	As a leader, notice if decisions are discussed but not decided. This is a role of your leadership.
	As a leader, notice how you are handling people who ramble, are excessively negative, or who won't shut up. The best way to manage some of these poor meeting habits is to give non-punitive feedback.
	As a leader, notice any off-topic conversations and side conversations and how you are dealing with them.
	As a leader, can you catch psychological traps, fuzzy or lazy thinking or biases, and keep them from hijacking the meeting?

✓	**Right before wrap-up** *The good meetings check sheet*
	As the meeting winds down, notice if people start to lose focus or drift off. Manage that.
	Ask if anyone has any related unfinished business needing completion.
	Ask people if they have done any of these: daydreamed, done other work, reviewed email, fell asleep, etc. You may not get an honest answer, but you will at least put them on notice that you expect them to forgo these behaviors in future meetings.
	Design a short survey to be administered at the end of meetings. Everybody answers some simple questions (names optional) which will be graded or tabulated. Post the results, and use the results for improving future meetings.
	At the end of the meeting, ask people if the meeting achieved the objectives and to write down any ideas for improvement.
	Some dimensions to question include things liked or not liked, do it differently or do it the same
	Thank everyone for attendance and any participation.
	Ask if this meeting causes any increase or decrease in stress in the rest of their job.

✓	**After the Meeting**
	The good meetings checklist
	Develop a system to follow up on tasks and responsibilities assigned at the last meeting (from the structure above). Then follow up on them.
	Publish brief minutes that highlight promises made, deadlines and follow-ups. Have a simple system to manage promises and requests. (This is related to structure above.)
	Consider creating a problem solving team. When the main meeting gets hung up on a problem, it can be turned over to a multidiscipline problem solving group. The topic will be tabled pending their discussion and recommendation.
	Add unresolved issues to the agenda for the next meeting. Bring issues forward from one meeting to the next until they are resolved. If any item is important, make sure it gets resolved with no further tabling.

Bibliography

Buterbaugh, Gary on his web site http://www.effectivemeetings.com/ including questions and answers from his blog, "The Meeting Guru."

Creighton, James L. and Adams, James W. R. from CyberMeetings © 1998 by Amacom, Inc.

Doyle, Michael and Straus, David. (1983). How to Make Meetings Work, Berkley Publishing Group, New York.

Effective Meetings (see Gary Buterbaugh). One of the best resources for people in or leading meetings is http://www.effectivemeetings.com/ . http://www.ehow.com/list_6639878_osha-safety-meeting-requirements.html has all the requirements for safety meetings in the US.

Gaertner-Johnston, Lynn, Tips for Writing Meeting Minutes, (January 05, 2006 blog http://www.businesswritingblog.com/business_writing/2006/01/tips_for_writin.html)

Galley, Mark "Cause Mapping Workshop," (2010, ThinkReliability)

Greengard, Sam. (1997). "Videoconferencing: Making the Right Connections," in Beyond Computing, [online magazine]; available from World Wide Web at http://www.beyondcomputingmag.com/archive/1997/11%2D97/connect.html.

Hanscom, Paul and Kathie Pugaczewki, PowerPoint on Board Meetings, http://www.slideshare.net/mach0072/effective-board-meetings.

Haynes, Marion E, (1997). Effective Meeting Skills, Crisp Publications, Menlo Park, CA.

Intelligent Meeting Management Company, http://www.iqm2.com/Default.aspx provides a meeting management tool from Agenda to Minutes. It includes follow up tools, tools for transparency for Governmental agencies and a complete archival system.

Kennedy, Beverly, Summary of the Robert's Rules of Order, found at http://www.robertsrules.org/ (1997, Robert's Rules Association).

Kieffer, George David, (1988). The Strategy of Meetings, Simon & Schuster, New York, NY.

Landmark Education is a training organization that offers several weekend and year long courses that enhance meetings. Titles include Communications Access to Power (weekend) and the Team Management and Leadership program (1 year). They have offices in most major cities including several offices world-wide. www.Landmarkeducation.com

Livescribe Smart Pen records audio and computerizes your notes. www.livescribe.com

Matson, Eric, (1996). "The Seven Sins of Deadly Meetings," Fast Company, online magazine; available from World Wide Web at http://www.fastcompany.com/online/02/meetings.html

"Meeting Minutes Format" Meeting Wizard Meeting Planning Center (no specified author) Meeting Wizard is a service of Codence Innovations Corp. http://www.meetingwizard.org/meetings/meeting-minutes-format.cfm

Meetings in America: A study of trends, costs and attitudes toward business travel, teleconferencing, and their impact on productivity A network

MCI Conferencing White Paper (no authors stated) (Greenwich, CT: INFOCOMM, 1998) now owned by Verizon https://e-meetings.verizonbusiness.com/global/en/meetingsinamerica/archive.php

Microsoft: Template for minutes and many other business forms and templates can be found at
http://office.microsoft.com/en-us/templates/meeting-minutes-TC001018411.aspx

Miller, Robert F and Pincus, Marilyn (1997-2004 revisions). "Running a Meeting that Works," Barron's Business Success Guides, Hauppauge, NY.

Nelson, Robert B. and Economy, Peter. (1995). Better Business Meetings (Irwin Inc, Burr Ridge, IL).

Okechukwu (Nigerian humorist and Motivational Speaker) can be reached at his Facebook page: http://www.facebook.com/ofilispeaks

Payne, Neil, "Business Meeting Etiquette" (Ezine Articles http://ezinearticles.com/?Business-Meeting-Etiquette&id=11774)

Parker, Sam. Blog post, http://www.givemore.com/

Penn State University, Building Blocks for Teams Student Tips; available at http://tlt.its.psu.edu/suggestions/teams/student/index.html#handouts and http://istudy.psu.edu/FirstYearModules/CooperativeLearn/CoopLearnInfo.htm

Plous, Scott. The Psychology of Judgment and Decision Making (1993 McGraw-Hill).

PowerPoint is the current world-wide standard for presentations at any kind of meeting. It is essential to build expertise in this essential tool. If you don't have time for classes, try the following free University tutorial: Florida Gulf Coast University at http://www.fgcu.edu/support/office 2000/ppt .

Richmeyer, Richard. Cartoon in blog post (October 2012, New Media and Marketing.com) http://newmediaandmarketing.com/

Richardson, Phil. Ground Rules List, prichard@faculty.ed.umuc.edu

Robert, Henry M. (1907). Robert's Rules of Order, Da Capo Press, Boston, MA. 2011 edition.

http://safety.blr.com/training/?type=62&topic=0 Safety newsletter and topics for safety meetings and toolbox talks

http://safetytoolboxtopics.com/Toolbox-Talks/ includes access to hundreds of safety toolbox talks suitable for industry.

Smith, Gary M. Etiquette (several journal articles) Chatgris Press in New Orleans. Titles include Peer-Reviewed Journal, Coffee and Coffeehouses and Cubical Etiquette http://www.chatgrispress.com/Articles/Business/Cubicle_Etiquette_Feb06.pdf . Gary can be contacted at gsmith@comm.net.

Streibel, Barbara J. (2003). The Manager's Guide to Effective Meetings, McGraw-Hill, New York.

Ten Commandments of Meetings. (Nov 01, 1999, no author noted). Reprinted from Harvard Business Communication: A Newsletter from Harvard Business School, For more information please visit www.hbsp.harvard.edu.

Weber, Ellen. Survey Your Meetings for Brainpower (July 25, 2010, blog) http://www.brainleadersandlearners.com/multiple-intelligences/survey-innovative-brainpower-at-your-next-meeting/

YAM (Yet Another Meeting). This is a great blog (2012, authors unspecified) with all kinds of research and statistics you can use when you want to convince management to improve http://www.yamlabs.com/blog/management_statistics_meetings/ There is also good information on their Facebook page: http://www.facebook.com/yamlabs

Index